FUNNY GYAL

ANGELINE
JACKSON
ith SUSAN McCLELLAND

WITHDRAWN

FUNNY
GYAL

My Fight Against
Homophobia
in Jamaica

DUNDURN
PRESS

Publisher and acquiring editor: Scott Fraser | Editor: Jess Shulman
Cover designer: Laura Boyle
Cover images: Jalna Broderick (bottom left); Reece Ford (top right)

Library and Archives Canada Cataloguing in Publication

Title: Funny gyal : my fight against homophobia in Jamaica / Angeline Jackson ; with Susan McClelland.
Names: Jackson, Angeline, author. | McClelland, Susan, author.
Identifiers: Canadiana (print) 20220140979 | Canadiana (ebook) 20220141487 | ISBN 9781459749191 (softcover) | ISBN 9781459750586 (hardcover) | ISBN 9781459749207 (PDF) | ISBN 9781459749214 (EPUB)
Subjects: LCSH: Jackson, Angeline. | LCSH: Lesbians—Jamaica—Biography. | LCSH: Lesbians—Jamaica—Social conditions. | LCSH: Gays—Jamaica—Social conditions. | LCSH: Gays—Legal status, laws, etc.—Jamaica. | LCSH: Homophobia—Jamaica. | LCSH: Gay rights—Jamaica. | LCSH: Lesbians—Identity. | LCGFT: Autobiographies.
Classification: LCC HQ75.4.J33 A3 2022 | DDC 306.76/63092—dc23

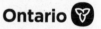

We acknowledge the support of the Canada Council for the Arts and the Ontario Arts Council for our publishing program. We also acknowledge the financial support of the Government of Ontario, through the Ontario Book Publishing Tax Credit and Ontario Creates, and the Government of Canada.

Dundurn Press
1382 Queen Street East
Toronto, Ontario, Canada M4L 1C9
dundurn.com, @dundurnpress 𝕏 f ⊙

To my LGBTQ and women's rights activist ancestors both living and deceased, I thank you for your strength and courage. I love you.

To LGBTQ and women's rights activists active, on hiatus, or retired, thank you. Be kind to yourself. Take the breaks you need. Find communities to support you. I love you.

To future LGBTQ and women's rights activists, I'm sorry this work still needs to continue, but thank you for taking up the charge. Learn about the people who have gone before you. Create communities. I love you.

To LGBTQ and women survivors of violence, I'm sorry. I'm sorry the world can be such a shitty place. I'm sorry you have to be strong. Do what you need to do to create healing in the way that is best for you. I love you.

To my direct ancestors, Grandma Pearl, Grandma Vernice, Uncle Anthony, I know you see me. I know you are proud. I know you love me.

For Sasha. I love you.

AUTHOR'S NOTE

This is a true story. All the people in this book are real. However, to protect identities, some names and characteristics have been changed. Dialogues have been recreated based on memory. Some liberties have been taken in terms of timelines.

FOREWORD

FUNNY GYAL FEELS LIKE A MEMORY AND A MOVIE. EVERY SEN-
TENCE VIVID. AND IN COUNTLESS MOMENTS, IT FEELS LIKE MY OWN
STORY. BUT IT ISN'T MINE. IT IS ANGELINE JACKSON'S STORY. WE
HAVE SO MANY TALES AMONG US WITHIN THE LGBTQI+ COMMUN-
ITY. UNBELIEVABLE STORIES AND ACCOUNTS THAT COULD NOT, BE-
CAUSE OF FEAR, B UTTERED BEFORE. SO THEY REMAINED UNTOLD
AND IN THE SHADOWS. FROM THE BEGINNING, ONLY THE ASSUMP-
TIONS AND LIES OF OUR EXISTENCE MANAGED TO TAKE ROOT. I AM
HAPPY TO B ALIVE TO WITNESS ANGELINE'S TESTAMENT.

I MET ANGELINE THROUGH A MUTUAL FRIEND, MAURICE
TOMLINSON, AN LGBTQI HUMAN RIGHTS LAWYER AND ACTIVIST
I GREATLY ADMIRE. I HAVE NEVER IMAGINED MYSELF AN ACTIV-
IST SINCE I AM EXTREMELY PRIVATE AND RECLUSIVE. BUT I ALSO
BELIEVE THAT EXPERIENCE AND TRUTHS R MEANT TO BE TOLD.
TO BE SHARED SO THAT OTHERS NOW AND IN FUTURE GENER-
ATIONS DO NOT FEEL SO ALONE OR AFRAID. I HONOUR, PRAISE,
AND TOAST ANGELINE AND ALL THE LGBTQ WRITERS OF POEMS
AND BOOKS, ESPECIALLY THE WRITERS OF THE REAL SHIT.

ANGELINE IS A TRUE STORYTELLER. AFTER ALL SHE HAS ENDURED, SHE STILL LEADS WITH LOVE, COMPASSION, AND HUMOUR. I TOTALLY RELATE TO "FUNNY GYAL" BECAUSE "MI FUNNY TUH." I WAS SHAKING MY HEAD READING THE WHOLE TIME UP AND DOWN AND SIDE TO SIDE, THINKING, "OH MY GOD! WOW! SIGH, YES! YES! YASSSSS!"

I HAD A GIFT THAT MADE IT EASY FOR OTHERS TO CONFIDE IN ME. IN MY JOURNEY, I MET QUITE A FEW WHO WERE ALSO VIO-LENTLY GANG-RAPED (CORRECTIVE RAPE) TO FIX THEM FROM BEING GAY TO STRAIGHT. IT IS A REAL "THING" THAT HAPPENED AND STILL DOES TO THIS DAY. JAMAICA IS HOMOPHOBIC WITH A RAPE CULTURE WITH DEEP ROOTS. DEEP ROOTS THAT LEAD BACK TO THE SLAVE TRADE, COLONIZATION, AND THE GENERATIONAL TRAUMA THAT, AS ANGELINE'S FATHER SAYS, "LEFT HOLES IN US." IT IS TIME WE ALL REGAIN OUR IDENTITIES AND POWER, AUTHENTIC POWER, THROUGH SHARING OF OUR STORIES, OUR VULNERABILITIES, OUR DREAMS, AND OUR LOVES. THAT WE SEE WHERE WE HAVE TRIPPED, NOT FALLEN, AND BECOME WHOLE, EACH AND EVERY ONE OF US.

I WAS TWELVE YEARS OLD WHEN I WAS RAPED. IT WAS TOO MUCH TO PROCESS. I DID NOT WANT TO B GAY, SO I BLOCKED THE ATTACK OUT. A SURVIVAL TACTIC. ONLY WHEN I CAME OUT IN 2012 DID I START TO REMEMBER EVERYTHING.

WATCHING ANGELINE WITH PRESIDENT OBAMA THAT DAY PUBLICLY SPEAK ABOUT US OUT LOUD WITHOUT OUTRAGE FROM THE AUDIENCE WAS A FIRST. I HAD BEEN HEARTBROKEN SINCE MY ORDEAL AND HOW I WAS TREATED BY ELDERS AND AUTHORITIES. I OFTEN REPEAT THIS QUOTE THAT I READ SOMEWHERE: "MY COUNTRYMEN BROKE MY HEART MORE THAN ANY LOVER COULD."

SEEING THE ACTIVISM WORK THAT ANGELINE AND OTHERS LIKE HER DO IS PERSONALLY HEARTWARMING AND GIVES ME HOPE. IT REMINDS ME OF A SILENT WISH I MADE BACK THEN AT TWELVE. THAT SOMEDAY, PEOPLE LIKE US WOULD GET THE COURAGE TO GIVE THE MUCH-NEEDED LIGHT TO WHAT IT IS TRULY LIKE TO LIVE IN SHOES LIKE OURS AND TO STAND UP FOR THE HUMAN RIGHTS WE DESERVE. SOME PEOPLE SAY A LOT, IN-CLUDING THE MORE LIBERAL-MINDED: "WE DON'T CARE WHOM U LOVE OR WHAT U DO BEHIND CLOSED DOORS." THEY JUST DON'T WANT US TO SPEAK ON IT OR TAKE UP SPACE. WELL, TIMES ARE A CHANGING, AND I LUV TO SEE IT.

I AM FILLED WITH GRATITUDE TO B A WITNESS TO ANGELINE'S TRUTH EXPOSED ON EVERY PAGE. *FUNNY GYAL* DESERVES LIGHT. OUR STORIES ARE VITAL FOR CHANGE. OUR STORIES R POWER-FUL AND VALIDATE OUR HUMANITY. OUR STORIES R NECESSARY TO FOSTER KNOWLEDGE AND TO IGNITE UNDERSTANDING AND COMPASSION. LGBTQI STORIES MATTER.

I WISH U ALL THE VERY BEST, ANGELINE. THANK U _/|_

DIANA KING

World-renowned reggae-fusion artist, singer, and songwriter, Diana King was the first Jamaican singer-songwriter and re-cording artist to publicly come out. They were born and raised in Spanish Town, St. Catherine, Jamaica.

PROLOGUE

For each of us as women, there is a dark place within, where
hidden and growing our true spirit rises ...

— *Audre Lorde, "Poetry Is Not a Luxury" in* Sister Outsider:
Essays and Speeches

April 20, 2015

I woke up before daybreak. I couldn't sleep much longer even
if I tried.

Weeks earlier, I had gotten an email from someone at
the U.S. White House who wanted to learn more about me.
President Obama was coming to Jamaica and was going to give
a speech in which he would recognize some young people for
the contributions they were making to Jamaica. I didn't know
who he would talk about, but in the days following I had received an invitation to the event, which was being held at the
University of the West Indies, Mona campus.

I am from St. Ann's Bay, Jamaica; breezy, houses painted in pastels, colours bleached from the sun that shines hot, except for those rainy, stormy days, often but not always during hurricane season, which runs from June through to the end of November. A place of contradictions: the same block on a road may boast a Christian Protestant Church — Baptist, Pentecostal, Anglican, Methodist, or Brethren — a stone's throw away from a corner bar, blaring 1980s and '90s reggae and '90s dance hall music, an offshoot of reggae with lewd raunchy words, from the component set. A group of men will be standing around a Ludo board, smoking cigarettes, drinking white rum and a chaser from six-ounce plastic disposable cups, a "Q" (two hundred millilitre) bottle of white rum in their back pockets.

Wooden homes and small flats sit beside newer larger homes made of concrete and steel, some as tall as three storeys. Many of these newer homes were built from the remittances of Jamaicans who live and work in the United States, Canada, and the United Kingdom. These buildings feature heavenly arches and wide balconies, and are shielded from the outside world by concrete walls or barbed wire fences and gates made from rebar steel.

One thing is consistent though: wherever one goes they are doused in colour — reds, pinks, yellows, purples, blues, oranges — and panoramic views of the aquamarine shallows of the Caribbean Sea. St. Ann's Bay is the capital of St. Ann Parish, which is known as the Garden Parish of Jamaica, because of our flowers, palm trees, and bushes, so lush, their outstretched arms form tunnels for cars and rivers to flow under.

Kingston, Jamaica's capital, a two-and-a-half-hour drive from St. Ann's Bay, is a place of contradictions, too. Modern high-rises sit beside old colonial buildings. The hippest, trendiest clubs, restaurants, stores, and hotels are streets away from inner-city communities.

The roads in Kingston were packed with more traffic than normal the morning I was going to hear President Obama speak. Or maybe it was because of the increased security around Kingston and leading up to the university that made it worse.

My taxi driver took a route I had never seen before, driving past Stella Maris Roman Catholic Church and heading into the hills.

"Angie, mi seh di road cork," my driver, a woman, exclaimed.

"Why? 'Cause a Obama?"

"Yeah, yuh fi si di mout a police weh out a road. Some road lock off and traffic divert all ova di place."

"Good ting yuh know yuh road dem!"

"Don't? So true, mi know seh yuh a go UWI and me know yuh haffi reach certain time, me decide fi come tru di hills."

We eventually made our descent back into Mona and approached the campus.

After the security check, I was directed to a seat in the second row directly in front of the platform. I looked around anxiously. People were starting to find their seats and the hum of conversation filled the air. I noticed a few members of parliament and activists from the Jamaican Forum for Lesbians, All-Sexuals and Gays, J-FLAG.

Lost in thought, I was startled by a tapping on my shoulder. I turned to see a U.S. Embassy staff member. "Are you Angeline Jackson?"

"Yes, I am."

"You're in the wrong seat. You need to move into the row in front of you."

My eyes popped open. *The front row?*

I began to feel the sweat dripping down the back of my long-sleeve shirt, which had the logo of the organization I co-founded embroidered above the left pocket. *I probably shouldn't have worn a jacket with this shirt in this heat.*

I hugged my backpack close to my chest and sat down. My hands were sweaty and I wiped my perspiring forehead with a tissue from my bag. I plopped three sticks of gum in my mouth, just to freshen my breath, then spat the wad out, wrapping it in my used tissue.

The president was introduced.

He walked out onstage.

I was sure everyone around me could hear the goat hooves that were my heart pumping.

I swallowed hard. I couldn't make out much of what the president was saying. Garbled. His voice. Like he was talking under water.

Please, no seizure, not today. Today is not the day this starts up again, I said to myself.

"Angeline Jackson is here today …" I finally caught what the president was saying. I looked down at my watch. He'd only started talking about six minutes ago.

You ever notice when you don't notice time, it's like it doesn't exist? As though there are pockets of space in between time that we fall into when we …

"Angeline Jackson … where is Angeline?" the president was calling out.

He was calling my name.

My head cautiously turned to the right and then left, seeing who this Angeline could be.

As I did so, I caught several eyes in the audience focused on me. I took a deep breath. On wobbly knees I stood up.

"There she is ... right there," President Obama said, with a smile that I could tell held behind it a giggle, like he knew, he recognized, my fear.

The president's face then became stern as he demanded the audience's attention.

"... as a lesbian, justice and society weren't always on her side ..." the president said. "But instead of remaining silent she chose to speak out and started her own organization to advocate for women like her, get them treatment and get them justice and push back against stereotypes and give them some sense of their own power. She became a global activist. More than anything, she cares about her Jamaica and making it a place where everybody, no matter their colour or their class or their sexual orientation, can live in equality and opportunity. That's the power of one person and what they can do."

CHAPTER ONE

Don't urge me to leave you or to turn back from you. Where
you go I will go, and where you stay I will stay.

— *The Book of Ruth*

Early July 2009

"Ova deh," I called out to Officer Smith, who was standing off
to the side talking on her cellphone. I kept pointing into the
clearing, hoping to get her attention. "A deh so it happen. Dat a
weh it happen." I was speaking Jamaican Patois.

I stared into the tall Guinea grasses where the man with the
gun and the beanie cap, wearing a bandana with a skull on it
over his face, had raped Sasha and me. The threatening storm
that had hung low and heavy on the day of the assault never
came, so the area was exactly as I remembered. Cedar, pimento,
macca-fat palm, and ackee trees framed the clearing and had

stifled our screams; not that many people came into the bush anyway.

I shivered then, remembering the cooing of baldpate pigeons and the squawking of green parrots. The hand, *his hand*, that smelled like gasoline and marijuana. The breath, *his breath*, stale alcohol, and his body odour, like he didn't bathe.

My being pushed down onto my knees. My being asked to …

I pinched my eyes shut and shook my head, forcing the vision to go away. "Mi did hav sum tings: tings he stole," I said to Officer Smith as she moved up beside me, her call having ended. "Mi waan luk." I started to step into the clearing, but Officer Smith grabbed my arm and pulled me back.

"Yuh cyah disturb the crime scene," she said. "Yuh hafi stan' back and look."

I wasn't sure what to make of Officer Smith. The male police officers, who had come on this so-called re-creation of the crime, sure made it clear they didn't approve of me. One short round officer had eyed me up and down with a look on his face as if to say, "Yuh sick mi."

I peered into the grasses for my phone, wallet, camera, money, and silver ring. I'd bought the ring in Ocho Rios. I wanted that ring back more than any of the other items. It was sterling silver and it had two steel bars across the front. I usually wore it on my index finger, but sometimes I wore it on my thumb, indicating to others in our community my identity: that I am gay. I felt the knot in my stomach tighten thinking of it. I bought the ring after Ana and I broke up for good. My body ached whenever I thought of Ana, because I still loved her. I wanted her back especially now, to hold me and tell me I would be all right.

It was all going to be all right.

Then my mind moved to Miss Campbell, a former tutor of mine with dark eyes she lined even darker in kohl. She only needed to look at me and draw me into her intense gaze. She had my full attention. She wore tailored tan and white cotton-blend suits, the pants of which would stretch real tight over her hips. Her ears she'd adorn in gold hoop earrings and she talked like every sentence was part of a poem. She told me she was a poetic justice campaigner, meaning she used poetry to advocate for change. Spoken word was her hobby. She made me come out to my parents before I was ready, but when I did, I bought that ring to celebrate, or to honour, or to just finally be. Daddy accused her of seducing me.

Oh, that summer ... those days now seemed so much simpler. Ana and our breakup, Miss Campbell, the older woman. I was seventeen and she was thirty-two.

"You were alone?" Officer Smith asked. I jumped, startled. My entire chest cavity tightened again, this time thinking of Sasha and what I had seen those men do to her. Sasha had begged me on the bus ride home to never tell anyone she was there. "What's the point of going to di police? Dem nah go do nutten. Dem a go mock wi," she had said. Her lips were moving when she spoke, but Sasha's eyes had stared out of her face, big and vacant. Her voice sounded like it was rising, limp and smoky, from the inside of a deep cave. The Sasha who had made me feel safe in the middle of hurricanes; that Sasha had left her body when the man, *the men*, raped her.

"Yuh were alone?" Officer Smith asked again.

"No, I wasn't," I managed to get out, knowing that unless Sasha came forward or I called her as a witness, the police wouldn't press for her identity. I turned to Officer Smith: "I can't see anyting on the ground but worms, ants, and grasshoppers," I said, changing the subject. "The man with the skull bandana probably already sell mi tings he stole."

"One of di men took yuh to a house afta," said a voice coming up behind me. "Show us." I turned quickly around. It was the short, round police officer wearing an expression of boredom. My face started to burn. I've been told my whole life that my level-headedness and calm made me appear older than I was. Although being an Aquarius, born on January 23, meant I was also, supposedly, forward-thinking and free-spirited. Regardless, inside, a storm brewed, *always brewed*, and it was set into motion when I felt anyone judging another person. There was a trauma there, that went way down into my belly. A wrong against me or anyone, I instantly saw as a wrong against all people.

Stifling my anger — I didn't want him to know he had gotten under my skin — I said I would lead them to the house. I slipped into the back of Officer Smith's car, while she and another policewoman from Spanish Town's Centre for the Investigation of Sexual Offences and Child Abuse, known by its acronym, CISOCA, and the policemen milled around talking. I blocked out their voices, to listen to the birds and to settle my spinning thoughts.

In the bush, back here, it was quiet, not even the sound of wind could get through in parts. We were not far from one of the highways that connects St. Ann's Bay to Kingston; a highway lined with tiny zinc-and-wood shops selling boiled corn, peanut cake, pink-on-top coconut cake, and gizzada. But in here, in the bush, there were no cars and buses swerving around potholes or honking at oncoming traffic. There were no women hawking roasted peanuts and candies from large wicker baskets. In here was silence, and I liked silence. I felt safe in silence. Psalm 46:10 says, "Be still, and know that I am God."

* * *

"That sodomite in the car ..."

My body twitched. I had zoned out, still tired, exhausted really, since the assault weeks earlier, but the short policeman's words dug their way into my thoughts and brought me back.

"That girl in the car, she a suh? She funny?" he said. I rubbed my eyes and looked. All the police officers, including Officer Smith, were looking at me.

My face grew hot again. I clenched my fists so hard, my knuckles hurt. "I am not a sodomite," I grumbled real low. For starters, sodomy refers to anal sex, so technically girls loving girls was not sodomy. But I knew in his mind, like on most of the island, definitions didn't matter: anyone identifying with LGBTQ was sick ... or what people refer to as "funny." I wanted to yell at that fat dumplin' of an officer to shoot me with his gun, that it would be less painful than the sting of his words. I tried to stare him down but the windows were tinted dark so he likely couldn't see me. He and the other officers turned their backs. I strained to hear what he said next. I picked out some sentences. "Like why are we wasting our time with that funny gyal," he said. He was wagging a chubby finger at me.

I slipped down into the torn upholstered seat of the Toyota Corolla. I kept chewing the inside of my mouth, this time to stop myself from crying. I closed my eyes again, focused on my breathing, and suddenly I remembered this woman I had met in the bush back when I was maybe eight. It was the very first time I'd gone into the bush — a bush that looked a lot like this place here but thicker, going on for miles and miles, moving into slow lurching mountains and gurgling streams. Daddy had quit teaching and was working as an insurance agent. He had this idea to move away from selling in the coastal cities where all the other insurance agents were tripping over each other, and sell life insurance to the people who dwelled deep in the middle of our island. The only way through the forests of palm and cedar trees was, in spots, by dirt paths. Daddy's bosses thought he was crazy, saying those inland people didn't trust governments or banks and likely didn't believe in insurance and wouldn't buy any policies. But somehow Daddy proved those bosses wrong. The people wanted life insurance; they wanted to have some security in case they got ill, and Daddy cornered the market all to himself.

I walked around as Daddy talked to his clients. In this one little compound of unpainted wood houses, I found myself skirting chickens and stray dogs. There was a broken-down rusted car. I peeked inside. It was home to a litter of kittens. When I looked up, coming up from a river was a woman. She moved until she was standing in front of me. My body became rigid, and I felt like I should scream. She put a finger to her lips and whispered for me to shush.

"Are you the Riva Mumma?" I asked, thinking of the stories Auntie Nora told about the lady spirit who, from the waist down, was a mermaid, and that some say guarded the treasure of the Spanish conquistadors. The River Mumma protects the waters, Granny Vernice, Mommy's mommy had once explained. All the things in the river, from the crocodiles to the fish, are her children. Without water there is no life and the River Mumma is a protector of life.

The lady in front of me wore a long white dress, so I couldn't tell if half of her was fish, and a white scarf tied around her forehead. There wasn't a hint of water or wet sand on her clothes. The woman's pupils were blue-white, covered in some film that made her not seem to be able to see. But while her eyes didn't appear to work, I sensed she saw everything. Her face was like a zillion years old, lined in wrinkles, deep like the cracks in a dried-up riverbed. I blinked to make sure I was seeing right. When I opened my eyes, the woman looked like my mother. I was about to run into her arms when her facial features morphed into a beautiful young woman. And then she returned to being old again.

She spoke. "You child, yuh goin' far." Her voice was crackly, like her insides were full of water.

"That's what my mommy seh," I said nervously. "Mi mommy seh I going travel di world."

The woman in white smelled like roses at dawn when their scent is the strongest. She moved in even closer to me and whispered in my ear. "It will be hard what you have to do," she said. "You will change how people look at things."

"How?" I asked nervously.

The woman stepped back and smiled. Changing the subject, she said to me: "In our storytelling, we weave our moments together like our grandmothers crochet a tablecloth. Our minds step forward and then gently move back, until we draw a perfect circle. When it is your time, you will tell such a circle."

CHAPTER TWO

A people without the knowledge of their past history, origin
and culture is like a tree without roots.

— *Marcus Garvey*

My very first memory involved a premonition. Mommy,
Daddy, and I were coming back from Sunday dinner at Granny
Vernice's house. I was not quite two years old, as I recall, but
memory, I know, is unpredictable. I could have been older, or
this might not have happened at all. Mommy's name, by the
way, is Miriam, and she is as quiet as Daddy, Emanuel, is loud.
Mommy and Daddy were both schoolteachers until Daddy
started selling insurance.

I was sitting on Mommy's lap on the bus leaving the town I
would later know as Portmore. Mommy was very heavy, pregnant with my sister Latoya. Mommy talked to her tummy like
Latoya had already been born, which made me mad. I wanted
Mommy all to myself. I had to curl my body around Mommy's

tummy now to nestle my face in close to her neck like I used to do.

My family and I lived in St. Ann's Bay, famous for being the birthplace of two of our greatest men, activist Marcus Garvey and reggae superstar Bob Marley. St. Ann's Bay was also home to the prison for the slaves that worked in the nearby sugar plantations. Mommy told me that while the prison was shut down, abandoned, many of the slaves still walked the jail cells as spirits, which we call duppies. "These are the slaves that died either in the prison or from overwork or disease in the sugar cane fields," she said. "Duppies are here because they have unfinished work, something they're supposed to do here." Mommy paused. "I hope you never see a duppy, for if you do, it means they have something they have to tell you, and usually what they have to say is a warning or a curse."

Mommy was a firm Christian. She read the Bible and, after getting married, devoted her entire life to the Brethren faith and our church, Bethlehem Gospel Hall. Most of all, Mommy believed in the helping hand of the Holy Spirit. Mommy sang church songs and prayed in quiet areas of the house whenever she had a moment to herself. But she would also talk about our island's superstitions, almost as though they held unspoken truths. Daddy said Mommy's entire family, who believed in spirits, were bak weh, meaning backward, which, as I grew older, I came to understand was not a good thing.

Mommy's family was big but Granny Vernice, Grandpa George, Auntie Rose, Auntie Sofia, Uncle Henry, and all my cousins lived somewhere else, far away, so far we had to take long bus and taxi rides to see them. But we did, whenever we could on Sundays after church. Before Daddy got a car, Mommy,

Daddy, and I would climb into a taxi that would take us to Ocho Rios, and then we'd clamber onto a minibus and then another minibus to Granny Vernice's house in St. Catherine. When I was little, it felt like we were driving right around the world.

On this night, the night of my premonition, it was really dark inside the bus. I could see nothing but the whites of Mommy's eyes. "What is it with you," she cooed. "You never sleep and like travelling."

"She will make a good wife one day, maybe become a teacher like us and like you, be a Sister in the church, teach Sunday school maybe, too," Daddy said. Daddy smelled like Brut cologne, Protex soap, and the outdoors because he liked to do a lot of walking. He was a short man compared to his brothers, my uncles Anthony, James, and Jonathon; neither slender nor stocky, somewhere in between, with high cheekbones, a broad nose, and big, dark eyes. He had the widest smile, too. Even in the dark, I could see his white teeth when he talked.

"Mi not so sure," Mommy whispered, pulling me in close. "This one different," she finally said. "She's come to move things around and move around." An image flashed in front of me of Mommy, but not like how she looked now. I knew then that Mommy and I had been together in a different life. I also knew I'd meet her, the woman she was or would be, in a future life. I had this feeling right then and there that I'd been here before, that I'd been someone else, and that I would be someone else after this life ends. Everyone around me had been someone else before and would be someone else after, too.

Suddenly, though, I felt a chill move through me. I started to squirm, wanting Mommy to let me go. I wanted to hide, because I saw in my own mind that Mommy was right. I would travel, and travel far. In fact, I would travel where no one else in Jamaica had gone, and I don't mean physically, like going to other countries. Yet I knew in that moment that the road ahead of me would not be straight but rather would have lots of forks and boulders blocking my way. I even felt the deep, crushing pain that some of those moments would bring.

* * *

The next memory I have, I was a bit older.

We had a few hours between church and Sunday dinner, which even when we stayed home involved a large meal of fried chicken, stewed beef, roast corn, baked macaroni and cheese, to-matoes, cucumbers, shredded cabbage and carrots, and maybe cake for dessert.

Daddy and I went for a walk. For a while, Daddy held me high on his shoulders and I pretended I was little Thumbelina, the main character in the book he read me before bed; dainty Thumbelina being carried on the back of a swallow up into the sky.

When Daddy and I reached the beach, he put me down. He started talking real serious to me, like I was already grown up. He said he didn't want to be like his daddy who had left when Daddy was real young and wasn't really ever present after that. Daddy said he wanted to be there for me and to teach me things about the church and Jamaica. "Today," he then announced, "is our first day of lessons."

I wanted to hunt for wilk, semicassis, and ark clam shells, but Daddy, a history teacher, told me to look as he pointed to that point far off over the water where the ocean and sky seem to become one. Daddy said that the Spanish explorer Christopher

Columbus once sailed there. Columbus came right up on these shores in 1494. Some believe Columbus was shipwrecked, others say that he just fell in love with our paradise. Either way, "here" didn't have a name then. So Columbus named it St. Ann's Bay Santa Gloria. Columbus and his country claimed not only Santa Gloria but the whole island for Spain, which owned it from 1509 to 1655. "The Spanish were the first," Daddy said with force, "to bring enslaved Africans to the island to work in the sugar cane fields. And don't you think for a second that Spain 'found' us. I never understood how colonists can say they 'found' and owned a place that already was home to other people." Daddy paused again and closed his eyes like he was thinking real hard or about to cry. "And in Jamaica," he picked up, "those original people were the Tainos, the name given to the South American Indigenous people, the Arawak, who settled in Florida and the Caribbean. Many of the Tainos were captured by the Spanish and, at first, made to work in search of gold. They were forced to convert to Catholicism, too. Many, but not all, died from diseases the Spanish brought over with them."

I wasn't that interested, nor was I really understanding anything Daddy was saying. If I couldn't look for my shells, I wanted the lollipops in Daddy's pocket instead.

Sevilla la Nueva or New Seville is where the island's first capital can be found, a mile west of the town of St. Ann's Bay, Daddy said. This settlement is said to be the oldest Spanish settlement in Jamaica and one of the first cities established by Europeans in the Americas. But the English came in 1655 and took over owning Jamaica from the Spanish. They further developed the sugar industry as well as a fishing port and built warehouses and wharves. "And to work the land, the English needed slaves, because the slaves already here had run away when the Spanish left," Daddy cried out. "The cycle was: capture people from the west coast of Africa, sell them to sugar plantations across the Caribbean, like Jamaica, Cuba, Barbados, who then enslaved them. All of our Jamaican products, like our sugar, went back to England. The first wife of King James II of England was Lady Anne Hyde. St. Ann is named after her."

Daddy stopped talking history for a tiny bit as we neared some buildings, a mix of old one-storey colonial wooden structures standing weak and timid against the surrounding new two-storey concrete buildings. We passed a bakery and a supermarket, closed because everything closes on Sundays, the Lord's day of rest. Daddy was walking fast, so I was running to keep up, and we didn't stop until we reached an old building, weathered and falling down like Auntie Titus, the ninety-year-old Sister at the church, who smelled like mothballs. Daddy pulled me up close to the building and pointed to the wood. It was full of holes. "Chichi," I said, using the Patois word for termite.

"The people who stole our ancestors from Africa, stole the island from the Spanish, who had stolen the island from the Tainos," Daddy continued. "Our ancestors were stolen people, kidnapped, plucked right out from their families, separated, and sent on boats on what is called the middle passage, from Africa to here. We're descendants of the enslaved people from West Africa," he said. "We're a mix of the Africans and Tainos." Daddy abruptly stopped talking. I looked up and saw his eyes now tearing and lips trembling. "Those foreigners gave us holes," he finally murmured, "like the chichi do the wood." Daddy stepped toward the building and ran his hand over the wood that the chichi had eaten. "Those foreigners," he said, in a quiet voice, "dug nails into our souls. We have holes inside us, just like our buildings."

As we moved through town, Daddy sang songs he said were from the church. I didn't recognize them, though, because his voice wasn't like Mommy's, which reminded me of the honey that I'd twirl around on my spoon. Daddy's "Do Lord Remember Me" sounded more like the taxi dragging its muffler that picked him up once and took him to work.

We walked until we came to the courthouse. There, Daddy stopped again. "Marcus Garvey was born not far from here," he said. I shuffled my feet on the dusty, asphalted road. I swatted away a fruit fly. I stood on my tiptoes now groping Daddy's pocket for the lollipops.

He pushed my hand away. "Listen to me, baby. Marcus Garvey was a great man," he said. "If you're going to travel like Mommy says, you need to know where you come from first. Marcus Garvey reminded us all that we are slaves to no one. He once said, 'A people without the knowledge of their past history, origin, and culture is like a tree without roots.' God gave you life, baby, but Jamaica is your roots that plant you deep into this earth. And what a strong tree you will be if you remember that. No matter what comes to you in life, you will prevail. I know that, the way God knows that. As Jeremiah says, "'For I know the plans I have for you," declares the Lord, "plans for welfare and not for evil, to give you a future and a hope."'"

* * *

After Latoya was born, Mommy and Daddy didn't seem to have as much time for me, so I hung out a lot with Rachel, a girl who lived down the road. Like me, she wore blouses and tops with long shorts that stretched down to her knees or skirts to her calves. Unlike me, she wore her hair in cornrows. Mommy twisted my hair into two-strand or maybe three-strand braids.

One Saturday late afternoon, Rachel came over to play house in my backyard. She got impatient and wanted to play skip rope instead. "Come with mi," she said, grabbing my hand. Her grip was weak. Rachel didn't have much meat on her. She was skinny like a palm sapling, so skinny in fact her knees and elbows jutted out like knots. I once had wondered if during a hurricane, she'd be swept away and I also wondered what fun that would be, in the eye of a storm; what would she see?

I pulled my hand back. "Nah. Look what I did," I said proudly, waving my now-free hand over the table I had set up for our dolls' tea party — a piece of tree bark for the top and four stones for legs. At the table, I had set Star, my pink-and-white teddy bear, and my Christmas doll. Beside my doll, Rachel had placed hers.

"Who's the daddy?" Rachel asked, stepping back and studying the table.

"They nuh have no daddy," I said. "Our dolls are both mommies and Star is their baby girl."

The dinner table that I had set in the sun was now hiding in the shade of a breadfruit tree. "Here," I told Star, putting a flat white polished stone in front of her. "Mashed potatoes and curry goat."

"A nuh Sunday," quipped Rachel with her hands on her hips. "You nuh eat food like this except on Sunday. Sunday, church day, that's tomorrow, not today."

I looked up. Rachel was squinting as she stared down at me. The skin on her arms and legs was mottled. She was cold. It was

Christmas season, which runs from the end of hurricane season until after the new year. This time of year, the nights become cooler, the days flood with a clean breeze — unlike after, when the air becomes soggy and humid and choked.

"You're cute," I said to her, staring at her big round face with freckles dotting her nose. I realized then I liked the feeling of her near me. "I'll play jacks if you like," I said. "But mi no want to play skip rope."

Rachel began to heave like she was a dragon about to spew fire. "Angeline Cecilia Jackson, you're not well," she eventually spat out, then quickly gasped and covered her mouth, like this was the worst thing she'd ever said in her entire life.

"What yuh mean?" I demanded, standing up quickly. I liked Rachel a lot, but she was prickly like an aloe plant.

Rachel shook her head. "Only boys play jacks and families always have a mommy and daddy, not just mommies," she said, her eyes now glaring at me.

Stunned, my mouth hung open. "I can do what I want," I eventually yelled back.

"There is something different and not normal about you," Rachel said in a low, haunting voice. She wiped her nose, which was runny because she was now crying. "Yuh not right in the head!" she shouted over her shoulder as she stormed off.

CHAPTER THREE

And the Holy Spirit descended on him in bodily form like
a dove. And a voice came from heaven: "You are my Son,
whom I love; with you I am well pleased."

— *Luke 3:22*

Daddy talked a lot about Hurricane Gilbert and how, when it
swept through St. Ann's Bay in 1988, it toppled mango trees
and breadfruit trees, some so much so, the top branches became their base, splayed out like spider legs. And the trunks of
these trees? They stretched up into the sky, like ladders, inviting
people to climb up to Heaven, like a kind of Jacob's ladder.

I don't know how, but most of those trees got turned back
around by the time I was born, the roots digging their way back
into the ground, but many of the trunks were still crooked, like
they were leaning over. Hurricane Gilbert seemed to be a point
in time that all the adults around me referenced. They would say,
"*Before* Hurricane Gilbert ..." or "This happened *after* Gilbert."

One of the first non-religious songs I remember listening to was "Wild Gilbert" by Lloyd Lovindeer. It was about the powerful winds that took the roofs off houses, and blew away satellite dishes. The song proved to me that Daddy wasn't exaggerating; that his stories, while often unbelievable, were, actually, true. Heavy rains had followed the hurricane and people, left without electricity in some places and without water in others, had to eat canned food for months, because crops were ruined and grocery stores destroyed.

For a while after I was born, Mommy and Daddy and I lived in a small house on a big piece of property that maybe, at one point, had had a large house on it. Looking back, I suspect this could probably have been the property of an English overseer, or merchant. The entire property was protected from the outside world by three tall cement walls. The wall at the front of the house had an iron gate that opened and closed and locked. The backyard was full of trees, including avocados, which we call pears in Jamaica. Mommy and Daddy were determined to be able to buy a car and a house of their own, and not necessarily in that order. Daddy was very hard-working, always talking about how in no way was he going to be like his daddy, who I gather didn't work much at all, and, in addition to leaving Daddy's mommy and all the kids, didn't send them any money either to get on in life.

After my daddy and mommy married and started a family, starting with me, he taught accounting at night school and did the accounting for two businesses in addition to teaching history during the day. Mommy taught high school math.

Not long after I was born, the Jamaican government changed the rules on the qualifications to be a teacher. Mommy, to keep her job, went back to college to upgrade her teacher's certificate to a diploma. At first, she commuted to Mandeville, which was about a hundred kilometres from our home. But the buses would often run late or not at all. When there were too many passengers, Mommy would have to wait, sometimes for hours, to catch another bus. So we all decided — and decisions in my family involved all of us — that she should stay in Mandeville during the week and come home on weekends.

To help us out, because Daddy was still working several jobs, Daddy and Mommy found a helper, which is the word we use for a maid, and Uncle Anthony, my daddy's brother, came to live with us. In part, Uncle Anthony was there to help out, but also it was a way for him to save money. Uncle Anthony worked as an apprentice in a hardware store. He was very hard-working, too. I guess he didn't want to be like his daddy, either. He wanted to own his own store one day — which he would, and that store would grow to be so large that he could afford a lumberyard attached to it. With Uncle Anthony now living with us, we needed more space. And that's how we moved from St. Ann's Bay to Seville Heights.

Our new home was the ground floor of a two-storey house, the entire front wall of which was made from cut stone. The house was owned by a Mr. and Mrs. Clarke, who were Jamaicans who had lived in England, earning salaries in British pounds rather than Jamaican dollars, and, because of that, were able to live comfortably in retirement. They lived on the second floor. The house had a big front yard and a concrete walkway lined with trees.

Even though I had a helper caring for me, it felt like I was being raised by two men. Uncle Anthony and Daddy would often give up on etiquette, plopping porridge or a stewed chicken still in their cooking pots right on the table. Sometimes we would use one fork or one spoon between us all; sometimes we would do away with utensils all together, and use our hands in a race to the bottom. Drool would drip down my shirt, which Daddy or Uncle Anthony would wipe away with my bib or a hand before I dug in for more.

* * *

Mommy eventually had three girls — me, the eldest; Latoya, two years younger than me; and Toni, born three years after that. All of us, for a long time, were raised by Mommy, Daddy, and Uncle Anthony, because Daddy encouraged Mommy's studying and career, saying his wife and girls should all have the opportunities to study and grow as people. So Mommy ended up getting not just her teaching diploma, but an undergraduate degree in teaching, and then eventually a master's degree in education. With each degree, she'd return to teach for a while, always earning higher salaries. Daddy, tired from all the jobs he was doing and wanting more time to be with us girls, started training to sell life insurance, hoping he could earn enough with just one job to support his family.

My life, all of our lives, revolved around God and Bethlehem Gospel Hall, dedicated in 1955, built on a third acre of land by members of the church and day labourers. Every Sunday there was breaking of bread or Communion, Sunday school, followed by family Bible hour, followed by Fellowship where all the adults milled around and got caught up with the gossip, while us kids talked among ourselves and played games at the back of the church building. As I grew older, Tuesday nights were Bible study and eventually Friday nights involved youth meetings.

Once Daddy passed the course to sell life insurance, he quickly showed his bosses he was just as good if not better than the veterans. In part, it was because Daddy could talk a sailor into buying a leaky ship if he wanted to. But Daddy was honest and saw merit in selling insurance to people the company had never considered as customers before. He used his first paycheque to buy an old dark-blue Suzuki Fronte, which he drove far out into the bush and mountains. Daddy became so successful that within a few years, he had saved enough money for us to consider moving to a house we would finally own and not rent. At dinner one night, he and Mommy announced to Latoya, then five; Toni, two; and me, seven, that they'd found the perfect plot of land. But they wouldn't buy it until we all gave our permission.

The next day, Daddy drove us girls out to see the place. Daddy parked his car facing a field covered in patches of swaying grasses and parched earth, and framed by bushes and pimento and guango trees. After a few minutes, I scratched my head and turned to look at Daddy, his right hand on his heart and his eyes lowered as if he was praying.

"But no house cyah build here, is only bush," Latoya said, scratching her head, too.

"Close your eyes and imagine your dream home right in front of you," Daddy replied, his eyes still closed, his lips parting into a smile. So Latoya and I both closed our eyes and did what he said. I guess, like me, Latoya saw a two-storey concrete home, with a wide verandah curving around the front and sides, a long driveway, and a garden full of rose and hibiscus flowers, because we both leapt into Daddy's arms and said we thought the land was perfect.

Mommy and Daddy then turned to saving enough money to build our dream house because they didn't want to borrow money and be in debt. I guessed this, too, had something to do with Daddy not wanting to be like his father.

Whatever the motivation, Mommy and Daddy said they had enough savings to move us from the Clarkes' to a home only we lived in, but we still rented, now in Priory, which was about four kilometres away from the centre of St. Ann's Bay. We'd live there, Daddy said, until our real home was built.

* * *

On moving day from the Clarkes', with Daddy, Uncle Anthony, and various Brothers from the church loading up our furniture in a borrowed truck, and Mommy and several Sisters packing our towels, linens, and china, Latoya, Toni, and I went out into the backyard to play. At one point, Latoya said she wanted to pray for a good move. I decided to pray with her. We both sat side by side, on our knees, hands in front of us in prayer and started with: "Dear Father God ..."

I loved watching Mommy's face when she prayed because I sensed a total surrender, like her cheeks and lips had been touched by Heaven itself.

On this day, I felt that, too. Heaven, I mean. I had this sense of a soft blanket hugging me tight, light and magical, and a warmth engulfing me. I instantly thought of the story in Genesis when, after He created everything, God looked at His Creation and said it was good.

I lay back and stared at the sky, fluffy white clouds moving on a blue sea. I thought of Uncle Anthony, who wouldn't be moving with us to Priory. He'd found his own apartment closer to his work. I thought of Daddy and how hard he worked to give his family everything. I thought of Mommy, when she would wrap me in her arms before bed, smelling of dish soap and singing me to sleep with church songs, her breath often still scented by the butterscotch candies she sucked on all day long. I remembered when she read to me as a child — usually children's Bible stories like "Jonah and the Whale" and "Joseph's Coat of Many Colours." Sleepy, I would slowly sink into her, not knowing where I ended and she started. That's how I felt about God on that day: I wasn't sure who was me, and who was God? As if I was in Jesus as much as Jesus was in me and as much as Jesus was in God, like John 14:20 says.

CHAPTER FOUR

The vision remains however, a united and strong front line
of LGBTQI human rights defenders, standing shoulder to
shoulder to stem the tide that erodes our freedoms.

— *Kenita Placide, LGBTQI and HIV/AIDS activist,*
campaigner, St. Lucia

Early July 2009

Officer Smith drove that Toyota Corolla police vehicle along the
path with the other cars following behind.

Beside her, in the passenger seat, was the other policewoman.
She was explaining to me that the purpose for these recreations
was to jog my memory in case there were things I had forgotten
that being out in the scene again, I'd remember.

I was in the back seat. The doors locked automatically and
though there were handles, I had a feeling they wouldn't work.
Despite the fact that I was a witness, I felt like a prisoner.

Officer Smith spoke into her cellphone, giving the location of the house, in case we needed backup. She said something like, "The assailant had a gun. Not sure if it was loaded. It was never fired according to the witness ..." After a short pause, she added, "He did not go with the witness to the house, but in case he was involved and ..." her voice trailed off, like the person on the other end was talking. Finally, she hung up.

I started to lean back in my seat. I wanted to close my eyes again. I didn't want to remember when I was first on this path. But Officer Smith asked me to lean forward and give her directions, the exact way we'd travelled on the day of the assault. I called out to continue forward, then to follow the curve in the road going left, surprising myself with my memory. I even recalled the exact place the man with the gun, who had been walking with us, suddenly disappeared. "So the other man, not the one with the gun, the one who took you to this house, said it was his grandmother's?" Officer Smith asked at one point.

"Yeah," I replied.

"But you never saw the grandmother?"

"No. Yes. I mean I never saw her."

"You must have been very scared," added the other policewoman, shifting her body and straining to look over at me. I relaxed a bit then. Like the officer who took my statement at the Spanish Town Police Station, a very pregnant Officer Cox, these women, unlike the policemen, didn't seem to be judging me.

"Yeah, we were really scared," I replied, forgetting to leave Sasha out of it. I caught Officer Smith, in the rear-view window, cocking an eyebrow. "I was scared," I corrected quickly. When the house came into view, I started to tremble. The peeling blue paint, the strained verandah in a bare, bleached wood, the wooden bench sent a wave of nausea through me. "I'm going to be sick," I said more to myself than to the officers. I'd been strong this entire time; I wasn't about to let them see me get sick. I pulled out a stick of gum, chewing furiously, willing the nausea away. But I couldn't escape the memory …

Remembering …

* * *

June 20, 2009

On the day of the assault, Sasha was acting differently. Distant, preoccupied, forgetful, which wasn't her. I had arranged to meet Foxxy in a more central and public part of Spanish Town. But since Sasha was with me, Foxxy and I set up a rendezvous that was more remote but closer to her home. "Yuh already coming up here," she had said, "it nuh mek sense me come down just fi come up back."

"Suh who dis Foxxy, again?" Sasha asked for the third time in the taxi from the Spanish Town bus station.

"Mi tell yuh already. I met Foxxy on the chat Ning, and wi been chatting for months. She seems nice. She's a friend," I reminded Sasha, who was perspiring more than usual. Her hands fanned her face, which was flushed, her cheeks fuchsia. Her smooth, dark almond-coloured skin looked pulpy, like she had some kind of fever.

"If yuh seh so," Sasha said, looking out the window of the taxi.

It was an overcast day, the clouds hanging low, keeping that stench of Spanish Town — gasoline, cooking fires, and garbage — closed in all around us. I went to shut the window, but stopped, knowing I'd be shutting in the stench of the inside of the taxi — previous passengers' sweat and odours from box food. I just wanted the wind to blow it all away. I shivered then. I don't know why. I just did. I wasn't cold. I was actually wearing too many clothes for the heat: black, heavy jeans and a thick grey and white T-shirt.

"Our stop," Sasha said, as the taxi slowed. She pointed in the direction of the roadside snack shop we were approaching. "Foxxy said this one, right? Around the bend from the ackee tree, just after the third intersection from the turnoff to the community?" asked Sasha, making me feel relieved; she couldn't be that ill if she remembered all those details.

"Yeah, dat she seh," I replied. "Foxxy want me call her when we get there."

"Mi nuh like the name Foxxy. Why she choose that for her online name? What her voice sound like?" Sasha asked. "Cunning, like a fox?"

"Nah, Foxxy's voice sounds nice. Real feminine. She never raises her voice, seems like the real thing. Says she's starting out as a schoolteacher at Spanish Town High School. I seen a picture of her on Tagged," I added quickly. "She brown, with a weave, straight and smooth, that makes her look posh. She look like a full femme. Tanks for coming wid mi," I then said, as we stepped out of the taxi into the humidity. "Storm coming, for sure, this is the calm before, when all the darkness just sits and broods. I hate Spanish Town, did I tell you that?"

Sasha nodded. Spanish Town was way south of St. Ann's Bay. Spanish Town was like the complete opposite of St. Ann's Bay. It was once a great city, built by the Spanish colonizers; it was actually the capital of the island, under Spanish occupation. It had the makings of a great city then, like Madrid or Paris. But the English, who kicked the Spanish out, made Kingston, twenty-five kilometres away, the capital, holding inside its parliament buildings our hopes, fears, wounds, and goals.

Spanish Town after that had morphed into ghettos and slums, some of the worst in Jamaica, maybe the worst in the world. And the crime ... it could be quiet like it was now, until 3:00, 4:00, 5:00 p.m. Then Spanish Town became a whole different city, with its underbelly of gangs and guns.

"You're quiet today," I said to Sasha, as we walked toward the snack shop. Sasha was usually a lot more talkative. While outwardly feminine, almost dainty, she could be dominant-like, too. She had a tomboy side to her. She loved football, which North Americans call soccer. Her slender hands would move like dove wings around the room and her face would light up when she talked about the latest football game between the Under-20 teams, or between Waterhouse and Arnett Gardens Football Clubs or Jamaica's national football team, the Reggae Boyz.

"Something just nuh feel right," she said, as she sat down on a bench. "Maybe I getting sick or sup'm."

"I can tell," I said, sitting beside her. "Maybe I shouldn't have brought you after all." As I spoke, I dialed Foxxy on my cellphone.

"Foxxy," I said in a loud voice. "Weh yuh deh? We reach. What now?" I was anxious. I wanted out of this place. Something didn't feel right to me, either.

"I'm cooking," Foxxy said, so loud Sasha could hear. Sasha rolled her eyes. "I going send mi brother who just come back from work, to get you."

"What? Mi come here fi meet yuh," I said sharply, my voice raised. "My friend Sasha is with mi," I said more quietly. "So you come get us. And what you mean, cooking?"

"I making you food," said Foxxy. "Mi brother cool. Him going get there soon and you come back for some fried chicken."

"KMT," I hissed, which means "kiss mi teeth." I punched the end button. I looked over at Sasha, who shrugged.

I shifted my feet, thinking about what to do. I was covered in dust from the trip. I moaned because I didn't like being dirty. When I looked up, I saw our taxi still parked by the shop. There had to be a good reason why the driver hadn't left, why he wasn't hustling to earn his fares, and I soon saw why. Inside the cook shop he was chattin' up a young woman, not much older than me, who was wearing an apron tied real tight to show off her curvy waist.

His remaining passengers, an old man and woman, were staring at him, willing him with their eyes to get back in the vehicle and drive.

I looked at my watch: 12:35 p.m.

I looked at the sky. A storm was sure coming. The clouds, getting lower and lower, greyer and greyer, started to drip around us, yet the sun shone through the clouds as though mocking them. "Hope her brother gets here soon," I said out loud. I felt deflated, like a balloon after the birthday party. I wanted to meet Foxxy so bad, but now that taxi looked pretty appealing, too, to be out of here before the storm. *We'd be home in an hour and a bit*, I told myself. "If that brother not here in ten minutes, we go. Okay, Sasha?" I turned to her. Her eyes were closed and her face tipped up toward the sun. "Okay, Sasha?"

"Yeah sure," she mumbled.

CHAPTER FIVE

Every day I get better at knowing that it is not a choice to be an activist; rather, it is the only way to hold on to the better parts of my human self. It is the only way I can live and laugh without guilt.

— *Staceyann Chin*

June 20, 2009

We waited on the bench, Sasha and me, for Foxxy's brother to come and get us. I was fuming, getting close to just grabbing Sasha and hopping back into the taxi, which was still idling.

Then Sasha stood up. "I think I see him," she said, pointing behind us to a dirt path.

"Where?" I squinted. I couldn't see anybody. "Maybe he took a leak," I said absent-mindedly. "Probably not him."

We both sat back down. Another shiver ran through me. "Did I ever tell you I saw a duppy?" I found myself asking.

"Why'd you think about that now?"

"Mi nuh know. It just popped into my head."

"Go on then," Sasha said. "Talk."

"Well, I saw it, a black shape, come in the front door before I could close it. It go through Mommy and Daddy's room. I follow and see it go into my room and then it left, out the front door again that I had left open. That was the same year I remember noticing time. You ever notice when you start to remember time? It's like as soon as you become aware of time, it gets shorter. As if time only starts when you notice it."

Sasha scratched her head. "No, I don't think I ever thought about this. Did you ever tell anyone about the duppy?"

"My aunt. Auntie Nora, Daddy's sister. You know her?" Sasha nodded yes. "Then you know she have a black spot in her eye. She said that black spot was from a duppy that she saw when she was in the cane field with Granny Pearl. That duppy came right into her, she said, and left a part of it behind; the black spot in her eye. I told Auntie Nora because I thought she would understand."

"Why you remember these stories now?" Sasha said. "You scaring me. Stop."

"You Dark Angel?" I heard a deep, gruff voice say from behind. I stood up quickly to see who was speaking.

"Who you?" I asked.

"Foxxy's brother."

I ran my eyes up and down his body. He was thick and short. I then stared into his eyes, the irises so black I couldn't see his pupils. He was black, not caramel brown like Foxxy, or even milk chocolate like me. No, even darker, like black coffee. I stood, planted my feet, hands in my pockets, and stared into his face. He squirmed like he had guessed, he sensed, that I didn't believe he was Foxxy's brother.

"Foxxy's stepbredda," he corrected.

I nodded slowly, thinking to myself *maybe*. Half-brother, stepbrother, a guy Foxxy called brother … whatever. "Come on," he said, turning toward the dirt path. "I will take you to Foxxy. Wi a go use a shortcut."

"No. Mi nuh do shortcut," I said to him, planting my feet. "Shortcut draw blood. I took a shortcut once and swore to never take one again. Let's go the normal way."

"Okay," he said. We started walking up the road, our sweat mixing with the gravel dust and sand and oils from the road making me real hot and thirsty.

We were just around the second bend and making our way up a small hill when Sasha stopped.

"I'm tired," she said. "How far?"

"'Bout twenty minutes. Less than ten minutes if we use di shortcut," this fake brother of Foxxy's said.

"Shortcut draw blood," I said real loud, just in case they didn't hear me the first time.

"Come nuh, man," Sasha begged, "twenty minutes a nuff time dat." She looked tired and annoyed and just miserable. I had to make sure she was happy since she was doing a favour for me. *Just this once*, I whispered to myself. "Where is this short-cut?" I asked the fake brother.

"Back down the road likkle bit, before we did start up di hill … on the lef."

So we walked back down the hill, nearing the snack shop where we had started. Smelling the scents of fried food, I realized that I was hungry and tired, too, maybe from all the anticipation or the heat. I really hoped Foxxy was telling the truth and had some fried chicken ready for us when we arrived.

We stepped into the bushes in single file with Foxxy's brother leading, followed by Sasha and then me. For the first little bit, it was like a jungle of long, untamed Guinea grass. When we entered a thicket of trees, some ground pigeons flew off.

It was even hotter and more suffocating inside the trees than on the road. It didn't take long before I felt like I was swimming in my clothes. But the sweat didn't bother me as it normally would, as much as this eerie feeling that we were being followed. I kept turning to look.

And that's when I saw it.

Saw him.

A man wearing a bandana with a skull on it over his mouth, and a beanie cap on his head.

He was holding, up high, a gun.

* * *

I swallowed hard and coughed. I wanted to call out and warn the others but the words wouldn't come. My throat was suddenly sandpaper dry. I pinched my eyes shut and then opened them again, hoping, *hoping*, he was just an apparition of an overactive mind.

But sure enough the image was still there, coming toward me, racing, and soon would merge on the path Sasha and I were on.

I must have managed some sound, because Sasha moved beside me and reached for my hand. The man coming toward us, pushing his way through ferns and tall grasses, was tall, and kind of thin, and brown, the opposite almost of Foxxy's fake brother.

I could see, as he neared, the handle of the gun was wrapped in green tape. My knees felt rubbery.

"Please God …" I began.

Foxxy's fake brother had stopped walking now and had seen, too. He stood frozen just like me and Sasha.

As the man in the bandana and the beanie cap drew near, that gun he had been waving around stilled, and got pointed at me.

I started quietly reciting Psalm 23:4: "Yea, though I walk through the valley of the shadow of death, I will fear no evil: for thou *art* with me; thy rod and thy staff they comfort me."

CHAPTER SIX

"I think it pisses God off if you walk by the color purple in a
field somewhere and don't notice it.... People think pleasing
God is all God care about. But any fool living in the world can
see it always trying to please us back."

— *Alice Walker*, The Color Purple

The summer when I was seven, the North Eastern Christian
Brethren Churches of Jamaica hosted an open-air crusade in
Ocho Rios. The congregations of all the Brethren churches on
the northern shore were invited to attend, including Bethlehem
Gospel Hall. The crusade was held for a week, on an open field,
filled with row upon row of plastic and metal fold-up chairs,
all pointing toward a makeshift stage for the visiting preachers and the church elders. There were sermons and services
every day, starting around six in the evening and going well
into the night. Surrounding the field were large speakers set up
to transmit the words of the preachers and amplify our singing,

because in every service we offer praise and worship to God through song.

I don't recall going for all seven days. I know for sure I went to three services, because it was on the third day that I felt it again, God, the Holy Spirit, or Jesus, the way I had with Latoya in the garden when we were moving from the Clarkes' house. It was at the end of the evening service, when the preacher opened his arms beckoning those to come forward who were ready to give their lives to God. "Anyone who wants to turn their life over to God and to serve Him, please come up to the altar," the preacher called out.

Then we began to sing.

> All to Jesus I surrender
> All to Him I freely give
> I will ever love and trust Him
> In His presence daily live
> I surrender all
> I surrender all
> All to Thee my blessed Saviour
> I surrender all …

I slowly moved toward the stage, like I was being drawn by some magnet.

"How are you going to give witness to Me in the world?" I heard the preacher say. "How will you help other people learn the Good News that Jesus died for their sins and that salvation was possible to anyone who answered the call?"

When I stopped at the front of the altar, I said to myself:

I am sure.

I feel this.

I am God's work.

I will do God's work.

After I answered *the call* and returned to my seat, Mommy stroked my cheek, while Daddy squeezed my hand and said, "We're so proud of you, Angeline."

"Mommy, Daddy," I said, "I'm ready to be baptized."

Unlike other Christian denominations in which babies are baptized, in the Brethren Church, members are baptized as adults, when they are fully aware of the responsibilities of dedicating their lives to God. Daddy had explained it to me this way: Jesus was not baptized by John the Baptist until he was man and ready to devote his life to God's mission of love.

Daddy scratched his chin as Mommy's eyes moved from mine to Daddy's and back again. "I'm not sure anyone so young has ever been baptized before in our church," she finally replied.

"I don't think I can baptize you," Daddy added. As an elder, he was able to baptize people, but I, being family, would have to be baptized by another preacher in the church.

"We'll have to talk to the elders," Mommy added, referring to Brother Jack and Brother Ridley. In my church, men were called Brothers, and were also considered uncles to all the children. The women were Sisters and all considered our aunts. It was like the church was one big extended family. "Are you sure Angeline?"

I nodded and smiled.

I knew. I knew in my heart of hearts, I was to be baptized. This was the path for me.

* * *

I grew up seeing the pastors in my church holding down other jobs. Uncle or Brother Jack worked for the phone company, and Brother Ridley, whom us kids in Sunday school called Mr. Wriggly, was retired, but he, too, had had a secular job. But church duties came first. When it came to my decision to be baptized, there were several meetings, and still the elders didn't know what to do since no one as young as me had been baptized before, as far as they knew, in all of the Brethren churches in Jamaica.

But they did allow me to start taking the classes to prepare for baptism. These classes took place on Sundays, at the same time as Sunday school. I left a large, loud class of kids talking in circles, flitting from how to perform the Bible story "Lost Sheep" to what kind of cake would be served at the afternoon Fellowship. Most of us wanted chocolate. Now, I was in a small class of quiet, focused adults, discussing and learning adult Bible stories, why we did baptism, and why we believed in the Trinity.

Our baptism class met in a room behind the altar of our church. Thick, heavy brown curtains separated the room from the church's main hall. Its only furnishings were two long, uncomfortable wooden benches and a few fold-up chairs. I sat on the front bench to listen to Uncle Jack, as he lectured about what the Trinity stands for (the unity of God the Father, Jesus the Son, and the Holy Spirit as three beings in one, forming the Godhead), and the role of Communion. The round hardo bread from Chung's Bakery down the road was blessed by the elders to represent Jesus's body. It was passed around during Breaking of Bread (or Communion), and everyone would pinch off a piece. When I was really hungry, I'd take a large piece. The grape juice, also blessed, represented Jesus's blood.

We spent several classes engaged in group discussions of what our roles as Believers should be. Most answered to spread the Good News, and live lives as an example of Christian living. But while the others talked about how they would do all of this — through prayer, through teaching — I didn't have an answer, only that God would lead me to my role when I was ready.

I wrote everything I could down in a notebook, sometimes using markers, other times pencil crayons. I paid more attention than I ever have in my life to something, wanting to show the elders I was just as ready for baptism as anyone else in the class.

About a month into classes, the elders still hadn't made a decision. During Fellowship, the guest preacher, Brother Mason, approached Daddy and Mommy to say hello. I was standing in between them, shuffling my feet, scuffing my white low-heeled patent-leather shoes. Brother Mason bent down and asked, "How are you going to do God's work?"

"Oh," I said, beaming. "I want to serve. I want to be an example to others. I want to be baptized."

The preacher, who was older than Daddy, chuckled, then stared at me, deep into the eyes, like he was trying to read something.

"I see your desire to serve God," he finally said.

"But I don't know if I can be baptized," I said slowly. "I might be too young."

The man straightened his back and turned to Daddy. "Sir, Brother Jackson," he began. "If Bethlehem Gospel Hall will not baptize Angeline, I will take her to my church and do it myself."

* * *

A week before my baptism it rained, really rained.

There was thunder, too. And lightning.

Mommy had invited my friend Annetta and a friend of Latoya's over to play. Mommy and Daddy were very strict about our playdates: no boys, and the girls' parents either had to be part of our church or friends of my parents.

Annetta was prickly, like I remembered Rachel to have been. The other girl, Latoya's friend, was chatty, almost bossy.

The four of us decided to play hide-and-seek. The other girl was it. She turned around, closed her eyes, and started counting to twenty.

I watched as Latoya slid under our little sister Toni's crib.

I could hear the other girl counting, "... sixteen, seventeen ..."

I ran fast, sliding as best I could on the terrazzo flooring, right into the room I shared with Latoya and then right under my bed, which was way lower than the crib. I pulled the bedspread down over the side so I was covered, and then blew the dust bunnies in front of me away.

I became real still and that's when I heard it: breathing. I wasn't alone.

I looked slowly, fearing a duppy, over my left shoulder into the face of Annetta. Her back was flush up against the wall, so even if the other girl peeked under the bed, she still might not see her. I pulled my body up close to hers so that our arms were touching. We listened to the girl calling out, "Ready or not, here I come." I inhaled the scents of Mommy's cooking that wove through every room in the house: scallions and thyme in the chicken soup that was simmering on the stove.

I thought about how I liked the way Annetta walked — back straight, knees kicking out, like she was a goat stretching her legs for the first time. Today she was wearing a red-and-white-striped dress with a red bow in her hair. I could feel her steamy breath on the side of my neck and it tickled.

I heard Latoya scream out: "I thought you'd never be able to find me."

My eyes followed a daddy-long-legs moving along the floor.

I felt Annetta, beside me, all warm and cuddly.

I turned my face toward Annetta again. Her lips were shiny, like morning dew on a sweet garden cherry.

I leaned in slowly and I kissed her.

"Found yuh," the other girl said, lifting up the bed covering, startling me.

Annetta squirmed, pulling herself away from me and then out from our hiding place real fast, like she was being chased by a snake.

When I was out and we were standing around, I could see Annetta was shaking. I was tingling all over, too. I felt flushed and excited and I wanted the other girl to go away so I could kiss Annetta again.

"Angeline did sup'm wrang," Annetta spat out, scrunching up her face like an overripe Otaheite apple, shrivelled and wilting.

I gasped and took a step backward. "Wah mi do wrong?" I demanded, very much baffled.

She puckered up her lips and blew me a kiss and that's when I knew. She didn't like the kiss the way I did. I felt the way I did when Daddy would toss me in the air as a small child. But this time, as I descended, his strong arms were not there to catch me.

I remembered Rachel, then, and how she had said there was something wrong with me. Flooding my mind quickly were the Bible stories that involved a husband and a wife: Adam and Eve; Sarah and Abraham; Isaac and Rebecca; Joseph and Mary.

As Genesis 2:24 says, "Therefore shall a man leave his father and his mother, and shall cleave unto his wife: and they shall be one flesh."

I thought of all the families in our church. Nowhere, *nowhere*, were there two mommies.

I shook my head and lifted my index finger to my lips, indicating for Annetta to keep her mouth shut.

When Latoya walked into the room, she asked what was going on.

Annetta, breathing heavily, repeated, "Angeline did sup'm wrang."

I wanted to sink into the floor.

"What she did?" Latoya asked. I didn't look up, but I knew she'd be glaring at me, her arms crossed and tapping a foot.

"Mi nuh biznizz," said Latoya's friend. "Let's play a nex game!"

"What shi do?" Latoya repeated.

"Figet it," said the other girl, grabbing Latoya's arm and pulling her from the room. "You girls an unnu gossip! Whateva shi did lets get anoda game in. Mi wah hide real gud."

Annetta, however, wasn't moving.

"Don't tell anyone," I whispered to her when the others had left. As I moved toward her, she took a few steps away. The lights flickered and lightning lit up the house.

"Nuh duh dat evah again," Annetta hissed. As Annetta passed by me to leave, she leaned in close and added, "You do that again, I tell your Pastor Daddy. It wrang what you did."

* * *

That week leading up to my baptism, after my kissing Annetta, I skipped meals, feigning I had an upset stomach and headache, which I think I really did have.

Daddy thought I was just nervous about the baptism. He then dove into a long speech about his own baptism and how scared he was. About whether he was strong enough to be a good example of God's love. What I dared not tell Mommy and Daddy was that I was questioning whether or not I was clean enough to be part of God's kingdom. I now had two girls telling me something was wrong with me.

As the day of my baptism drew near, I began silently asking God whether I should be baptized or not.

"Please … give me a sign, any sign, that you want me to be baptized, that this is your calling for me?"

The night before my baptism, I barely slept. I woke so early it was still dark out. I could hear the night sounds of the lizards, croaking to each other.

I was shaking and cold. I got out of bed to close the window.

As I reached for the handle, I suddenly forgot what day it was. I felt warm and comfortable. I stood motionless listening to the sound of Latoya's quiet breathing and the stillness of our house.

I turned and looked around my bedroom, my eyes stopping on the open closet door. Hanging from a hook was my white baptism dress.

I closed my eyes and started singing "Create in Me a Clean Heart," a church song, ever so softly so as not to wake Latoya. When done, I opened my eyes and looked out the window. The top rays of the sun were pushing their way over the land.

Can God talk through the rays of the sun? I wondered. Is this the answer to my question?

Almost as if in response, beams of sunlight moved into the bedroom, landing on my dress, illuminating it.

"Thank you," I whispered. "Thank you, God. I am in your hands, guide me as you desire."

CHAPTER SEVEN

I can do all things through Christ who strengthens me.

— *Philippians 4:13*

June 20, 2009

After,

    after Sasha,

    after me,

    after the two men had us do things to them,

the man wearing the bandana with the skull on it and the beanie cap and carrying the gun ordered us to walk: Foxxy's fake brother first, Sasha second, and me third, the barrel of the gun pressing against the back of my neck.

I could hear Foxxy's fake brother ahead of us, puffing. I continued to pray. I was not sure I'd ever stopped.

At some point I recalled something Daddy had told me:

"God never gives us more than we can handle." And telling myself, I can handle this.

The gravel crunched under my feet. I heard a bird chirping and the braying of a donkey in the distance and the creaking of banyan trees.

"He's gone," called out Foxxy's fake brother.

Sasha and I kept walking. "He's gone," Foxxy's fake brother said again.

I slowed my gait and turned my head, anticipating that gun would now be pointed right at my face. But Foxxy's fake brother was right. The bandana-man was nowhere in sight.

"Sasha, it's okay, he's gone." She must have been expecting to be shot, too, because her body was trembling and her head was buried down low in her neck the way mine had been.

"I'm sorry I brought you ..." Foxxy's fake brother began, then stopped. He was acting like he wasn't involved, like the man with the bandana had forced him to rape Sasha and forced me to perform sex acts on him.

Sasha moved up beside me and slipped a perspiring hand into mine. I looked deep into her dark brown eyes. Sasha had always had the most beautiful eyes — big, round, with long eyelashes. The whites now were crimson, lined in red veins.

My body twitched and I started to move toward Foxxy's fake brother to let him have it. Sasha pinched my hand hard, holding me back. She then shook her head quickly. "Don't," she whispered. "We need to get out of here. He may be on our side, an innocent in this, or guilty. He did things to us, too. Either way, we get to a safe place first."

"I had nothing to do with this, yuh haffi believe mi," Foxxy's fake brother said, as if he had overheard. His voice was high-pitched now, not what it was when we first met him, like he was nervous, desperate. "That was so bad," he added quickly, shaking his head, like what was done to us was done to him as well.

"He stole our phones and money," Sasha said to him. "How do we get home?" Her voice was composed, controlled. I marvelled at her strength.

"My grandmother lives up the road," Foxxy's fake brother said, hands now in his pockets and his head lowered like he was ashamed. "Come with me. You can clean up there and call Foxxy. She may know what to do."

I started to shake my head no. No way am I following you, you rapist. But again Sasha squeezed my hand hard and held me back from jumping on him.

"You lead," she said to Foxxy's fake brother.

As we walked, I began to get angry at myself. The bandana man was wimpish, and I am a strong, heavily built girl. If Foxxy's fake brother really wasn't in on it, we could have overpowered him. But then the assault was too orchestrated, I told myself. The bandana man was running ... running right toward us, like he knew where we would be. Foxxy's fake brother had to be involved. He had to have set it up.

The three of us walked until Foxxy's fake brother stopped in front of a small weather-beaten home made of wood. He told us to wait outside, at the gate, while he talked to his grandmother. Sasha and I huddled in close together, our eyes glued to the back of his head as he moved up the groaning wooden steps, opened the door, creaking on its hinges, and then slammed it shut.

I pulled Sasha in even closer. "What if this is another trap? What if we go in there and there are more men waiting for us?"

"I know. I know," she said, shaking her head. I bit my lip to stop myself from screaming. I wanted to raise my hands and shout, "I surrender! Just please, *please*, leave my friend alone. Do what you want to me."

"Play along," she said. Sasha was in survivor mode and clearly taking control. "We've seen his face. He might kill us, if he thinks we're going to go to the police. Just act like he's innocent. Act like it's all okay. That we just want to go home"

Foxxy's fake brother appeared in the doorway. "Grandma's not home," he said. "But come in. You'll be safe here while we figure out what we should do." As Sasha and I inched toward the door, I strained to listen for voices, the sound of movement, a thud, anything to indicate that behind Foxxy's fake brother were more people. I looked up at the sky and figured from the light it was about 2:00 p.m.

I made a mental note to write down everything I could remember as soon as I had a pen and paper. Sasha's resolve had shifted my mind into analytical mode. I was now gathering evidence in my head: evidence to take to the police.

The inside of the house was dark and musty, the air heavy with the scents of kerosene and cooking oils. Sasha and I didn't sit down at first, despite Foxxy's fake brother waving a hand over a battered couch. We stayed close together at the front door, in case we had to make a run for it. Foxxy's fake brother passed us his phone that the bandana man had not stolen. Neither of us reached for it.

He took the phone back and punched in a number. A picture of Foxxy showed up on the screen. Angrily, I grabbed the phone, breathing heavy now, my blood boiling.

"Where you?" I yelled as soon as Foxxy came on.

"I waited," she said in that smooth, honey-like voice that had made me want her so bad. Now that voice sounded ugly, coarse, and manipulative. "So when you didn't come, I went out to buy some sandals."

"What?" I said with a gasp, knowing I had heard her well enough. I just needed her to repeat what she had said, I was so much in shock.

"You didn't hear me? Mi leave fi buy shoes. Yuh a come or not? It late now. Maybe we should meet up another time."

"Yuh a idiot?! How yuh fi lef yuh house when yuh done know seh yuh bredda did come fi wi and we were on our way? Yuh lick yuh 'ead? How yuh fi leave di house, fi buy fucking shoes? A weh di bumboclaat! Yuh mad? Why di rass mi wuda come back?" I ranted. Foxxy's fake brother reached for the phone back. I hit his hand away. Sasha patted the back of my arm indicating for me to calm down.

"Okay," I heard Foxxy's voice coming through the phone. "Gi mi bredda back di phone."

I looked over at Sasha who had moved to the couch and was sitting down, bent over at the waist. She was holding her abdomen like it hurt. Her head was lowered, her shoulders slumped, and her legs pulled in tight together.

Foxxy's fake brother went outside to talk to Foxxy. I sat down beside Sasha.

"You all right?" I asked.

"I'm bleeding," she whispered.

I looked around the dimly lit house. "I think it's safe to use the washroom."

Before Sasha could decide what to do, Foxxy's fake brother was back, standing in front of us. "I'm going to go down the road, to a friend's place, and get some money for you," he said. "Foxxy says for you to wait here. I'll be back soon."

He was then gone, out the door; Sasha and I sitting, listening, to the pounding of his feet, running in the opposite direction of us. Sasha finally pulled herself up. As she limped toward the back of the house and where she hoped was a washroom, she faltered, placing a hand on a table to steady herself.

I sat there, straining to hear any unusual sounds, as she turned on a faucet. A few minutes later, she returned, holding her bloody underwear. I took them, without a word, and put them in my now empty backpack. The only thing the guy in the bandana didn't take was an open pack of chewing gum.

"Evidence, you know," I said to Sasha, who was eyeing me. "Your panties are evidence." Her body flinched then. She swivelled her body so she was facing me.

"I don't want to go to the police," she said. "I just want to go home. This never happened."

* * *

Foxxy's fake brother returned and gave us some money for the bus; that bus ride home, hurting and lost, Sasha said few words except, "Promise me if you go to the police, you won't tell anyone I was there? Promise me?"

"Yes," I reassured her. "Yes."

When we got back to St. Ann's Bay, she disappeared into the night and I made my way home, not thinking, my thoughts somehow dulled, my body not feeling like it belonged to me.

As I approached my house, I slowed. Daddy's car was not in the driveway. He was probably picking up Latoya from the library and Toni from a program at church. But Mommy would be home, waiting for us, perhaps marking papers at the kitchen table. Or maybe she was dozing while dinner cooked, the gospel radio station, Love 101, playing softly on the radio.

I moved closer to the house, until I was standing near the side door. As I reached for the handle, suddenly, like a switch, my mind turned on again and I saw everything that had been done to Sasha and me as if in real time, as if I was a spectator, not a participant. Instead of seeing my face, however, I saw all the faces of the people I had met volunteering with Jamaica AIDS Support for Life, known as JAS or Jazz, depending on who you asked. The broken bones, the tired eyes, the sagging spirits.

Anger stewed inside me.

"Raas," I said out loud using the swear word we commonly use.

I pulled open the door and stepped into my house.

CHAPTER EIGHT

Definitions belong to the definers, not the defined

— *Toni Morrison*, Beloved

In the house we were renting in Priory, there was an alcove in between the bathroom and our bedrooms. Mommy and Daddy had placed a bookshelf there. The bookshelf itself had glass doors that, while always shut, had a key sitting in the lock.

I'd only ever been interested in the history and geography books. But the summer before I was to start Grade 5, I found myself drawn to the other books, like something was calling out to me, but I didn't know what.

I had turned ten that previous January, and with that birthday came an almost overnight dislike of playing dolls and make-believe with my sisters, instead wanting to be alone, and reading.

One lazy afternoon, when my sisters were watching endless hours of cartoons on the small colour television Daddy had bought in Ocho Rios, and Mommy was preparing a brown stew chicken for dinner, I crept to that nook and stood in front of the bookshelf.

I ran a finger along the tops of the books, pushing up dust. Then I stopped, I don't know particularly why, my finger atop a book with a yellow spine. I tilted the book on its side and saw that the cover, half torn off, was bright yellow, too.

I pulled the book out slowly and read the title page: *Everything You Always Wanted to Know About Sex, But Were Afraid to Ask.*

My eyes grew wide and I felt a rush of both intrigue and fear move through me as I pulled that book out and tucked it inside my blouse. I then scurried on tiptoe to my bedroom.

I shut the door.

I turned off the lights.

I listened. No one was coming.

I pulled the book out from underneath my blouse and crept to my bed, grabbing the small flashlight I used late at night to help me read when my sisters were sleeping.

I crept under the covers.

I stopped on the contents page, my heart pounding.

"Beyond the Birds and Bees."

"Male Sexual Organs."

"Female Sexual Organs."

"Impotence."

"Frigidity."

"Male Homosexuality."

"Masturbation."

"Sexual Perversion."

"Prostitution."

That very first day, I learned words like *aphrodisiac*, which was a drug taken or mixed with food or a drink to arouse someone sexually. I read about how wives were being slipped Spanish fly, or cantharidin, a drug extracted from dried and pulverized iridescent beetles to become sexually aroused.

I learned about female and male sexual anatomy. Who knew we girls had three holes?

When not at home or sleeping, I tucked the book in between my mattress and box spring. And when my sisters read out loud from their picture books, I devoured every page of the yellow book in my private tent under the covers, a thirst overwhelming me, like I had had for only one other book before: the Bible.

The yellow book, as I came to call it, addressed the stages of sexual awakening and said that in childhood, we are interested in each other's bodies, including girls interested in other girls, and boys, boys. I translated that into the reason I had kissed Annetta. I was exploring, according to the book, a healthy stage in development.

I also learned about masturbation, and in the quiet hours of the morning, I would touch myself, feeling that heat of pleasure moving through me as I found my clitoris and realized that simply applying intermittent pressure for a few minutes would make my whole body tense and my toes curl for a few seconds.

There was a chapter on sexual perversion, which the author, a doctor, who apparently had consulted with other doctors, described as any person not interested in "penis-vagina sex." People who wanted to have sex with others of the same gender, according to the doctors, were stuck in infantile stages of sexual awakening. These people never grew out of the urges of childhood. This chapter described transvestites and homosexuals as sexual deviants. Male strippers were peeping Toms. Female strippers were paid peeping Toms. Female homosexuals were prostitutes.

I knew the word *prostitute* from the stories of Mary Magdalene I had heard on Bible radio shows. She was the sinner washing Jesus's feet and the woman cured of seven demons in the Gospel of Luke. The Old and New Testaments outlawed prostitution, starting with the Hebrews, who really banned it for Hebrew women but seemed okay with non-Hebrew women being prostitutes. Prostitutes were sexually immoral, unfit for Heaven.

All interesting. Fascinating really.

Reading on perversion, it was there that I would first come to learn of the word for girls who liked girls, women who had sex with women: *lesbians.* According to the yellow book, a lesbian fell into one of several categories:

- a "Dyke: a prostitute who is a lesbian with masculine characteristics";
- a "Bull dyke: a dyke, but even more masculine";
- a "Butch: same as dyke";
- a "Femme: a feminine appearing lesbian prostitute"; or
- a "Lezz: any lesbian prostitute or female customer."

I snuck the yellow book into the Ecumenical Bible Camp, a week-long sleepover camp held in a high school. At one point, I pulled my friend Chevelle aside and asked her if she knew if there were Bible passages that directly addressed males being with males, females with females? Of course, we all had our Bibles with us. Summer holidays from school were filled with Church activities, starting with vacation Bible school held at

Bethlehem Gospel Hall, during which we'd learn Gospel passages, and make arts and crafts, like Jesus's cross from wooden craft sticks. We'd also put on plays such as Joseph and his coat, and the Prodigal Son.

Chevelle and I drifted away from the rest of the group. Huddled close together in a back hallway, constantly checking to make sure no one was coming, she told me what she knew about the passages that spoke about homosexuality (which we eventually learned were called the clobber passages or verses). While we could not recall the preachers at our two churches talking directly in their sermons about same-sex relationships, Chevelle said that the clobber passages were verses in the Bible that churches, including our own, used to ban same-sex relationships. One such passage was in Leviticus, Chevelle showed me, which says, "Do not lie with a man as one lies with a woman; that is detestable" (Leviticus 18:22), and "If a man lies with a man as one lies with woman, both of them have done what is detestable. They must be put to death; their blood will be on their own heads" (Leviticus 20:13).

At the end of that summer, I slipped the yellow book back into its place on the shelf, relieved Mommy or Daddy hadn't noticed it missing, my mind a tumble of weeds of everything I had read and learned that summer. Most of all, I clung tight to the section in the yellow book on sexual maturity. My helping the boys at my school look up the girls' skirts by installing mirrors under their chairs was just a stage I would move beyond. I was normal. I was not a deviant. I was none of the things Annetta and Rachel had called me.

* * *

Butch/Stud: in the lesbian world, a woman who displays and performs roles that are typically associated with men

Stem: a woman who expresses and operates somewhere between the femme and butch extremes (stud + femme = stem)

Femme (in Jamaican butch/femme dynamics): a woman who behaves and presents herself in stereotypically feminine ways, usually lacking any significant masculine characteristics

January 2009

I wanted to meet other girls like me.

Having desires and having been with Ana and Miss Campbell, I wanted to kiss girls that wanted to be kissed and held and touched like I did. But this was Jamaica and there were no clubs or sections of cities like in North America and Western Europe where lesbians, gays, and bisexuals could meet each other. I was attending GLABCOM (Gay, Lesbian, Allsexual, and Bisexual Community) meetings in Ocho Rios, but I was almost always the only female. After a discussion on safe sex, we'd party, to hip hop and dance hall music.

My gay friends told me that Digicel, one of the telecommunications providers, had text-based chat rooms, at least two of which were for lesbians. Sasha told me about the one she was in and gave me instructions on how to join. All I had to do was text LESBIAN to CHAT (2428). Or, if I wanted to see if there were other related chat rooms, I could text LIST to CHAT (2428). I joined two chat rooms: LESBIAN and GIRLS4GIRLS.

In the chat rooms, it seemed, the users were either femmes or butches. If someone was in between, no one really took them seriously. Bisexual women seemed to disgust the others, who would post about what a turnoff it was to envision a penis going into the same vagina they were tasting.

The butches would post about the type they were looking for: "slimmaz," meaning slender, short, brown, pretty hair, submissive, funny, loves sex," or "not taller than 5′ 7″, DDD breast size, big butt, can handle a strap-on." The femmes: "athletic body, brown skin, can handle business attitude (determined, financially resourced)."

An example of a post: "5 foot, brown skin, living in Portmore, looking for a 'soft' butch, must have a job, looking for something long term. Text 381-0000."

I remained silent in the chat rooms for a while, watching the messages and how people spoke or wrote and interacted with each other. I also hadn't thought about whether I was a femme or a butch, and I wasn't sure how to describe myself. I wasn't sure of my height. So I started off quiet, a ghost, almost stalking, checking the chat rooms multiple times a day to see if anyone had posted a profile that either informed me how to describe myself or looked interesting enough for me to text and engage in a conversation.

Sasha also introduced me to Rainbow Vibes, on the social network platform Ning, which was free for users. Rainbow Vibes was online, so I could log out and clear my search and chat histories, which the chat rooms didn't allow me to do. I could screen girls and women not just from the words they posted but by their profile pictures, too. I could know what they looked like from the moment we started talking.

I eventually described myself as a soft butch, meaning I wasn't a butch but had butch tendencies in relationships. I decided to use the name Darkangel, from the TV show of the same name, because I was very much into strong female fictional characters like Buffy the vampire slayer and Xena the warrior princess.

I met Foxxy on Rainbow Vibes. I sent the initial message to strike up the conversation:

"Hey Foxxy, I noticed your profile picture. You have a cute smile and I wanted to get to know you."

"Hi Darkangel," her message a few days later said. "You have a cute smile, too."

Our conversations were short and inconsequential, sharing descriptions about our days, what we did — for me, it was mostly studying, going to school, and reading the Bible.

Then one day the tone of the conversations changed.

"I want to kiss your neck and squeeze your breasts," I typed. I don't know what came over me. I wanted to take the words back. I was sure Foxxy would ignore me. I mean, she was beautiful. She was probably talking to many girls. I waited and waited, for the longest time — okay, it was only a few hours, maybe minutes — for her to reply.

I paced the room. I bit my nails.

"I'd love to feel your hands on me, feeling my nipples harden and press against the palm of your hand," she replied. "If you came to Spanish Town we could spend some time together. We could see what we get up to."

"I don't like Spanish Town, Foxxy, I'm not interested in going there."

"I don't live in Spanish Town proppa. I live on the outside, one of the safer areas."

"What would you give me to make it worth my while?"

"Well, I could cook for you. I know you like someone who cooks. We don't even have to have sex, though I really want to kiss you and want you to touch me."

Feeling the heat rising between my thighs, desperately wanting to taste her lips, I wrote, "I'll think about it," knowing full well that my body had already said yes.

CHAPTER NINE

Who we are cannot be separated from where we're from.

— *Malcolm Gladwell*, Outliers: The Story of Success

June 20, 2009

I'm inside my house, hours after the assault, but it felt like I'd been away for years.

I moved into the living room.

No one was there.

I walked toward my parents' bedroom, seeing the door ajar.

In front of the door, I stopped again and listened. Not a sound. Mommy had to be asleep. She often took naps before dinner, when she had the chance. When no one was home.

Should I wake her?

I thought of my sisters, imagining what happened to me, to Sasha, happening to one of them.

I pushed the door open, moved toward Mommy's side of the bed, turned on the light, and shook her shoulders until her eyelids fluttered.

Mommy sat up, blinking as her eyes adjusted to the light.

And then terror took hold of her face: her eyes widening, the lines on her forehead furrowing, her mouth opening and closing, like she was talking, but no words came out.

She grabbed my hand hard, and pulled me down beside her.

"What happened?" she finally got out.

"I've been attacked."

Mommy said nothing for the longest time, but I knew in her head she was saying a lot to herself.

"I'm calling Uncle Sam," she eventually said, referring to a relative whose niece worked at the police station in nearby St. Mary. Mommy reached for her cellphone and then stopped. She faced me, her eyes softening.

"Is this what you want, Angeline?" she asked.

I nodded yes.

* * *

Uncle Sam's niece contacted the CISOCA unit in St. Ann's Bay. A female police officer called Mommy's cellphone. After asking me a few questions, the police officer said she was on the way over to the house.

Mommy and I waited, silently, just holding hands, Mommy looping a finger on top of my palm, stroking it softly. "Why do people hate?" I wanted to ask her. "Why do people hurt other people? Why is there evil?"

Instead, I leaned into her, like I did when I was a child. I
wanted to feel like we were one again. I wanted to recall that
sensation of not knowing where she started and I ended.

After a while, Mommy began humming "As the Deer
Panteth for the Waters."

She was, in her way, letting me know that it was not her I
should rely on, but God.

* * *

By the time the police officer arrived, Daddy was home. Mommy
had snuck away to tell him what little she knew, and to explain
to my sisters to stay in their rooms. I heard Mommy preparing
them some dinner, then her slippers shuffling on the tile, the
tinkling of glass and cutlery, and the whispered conversation as
she handed my sisters trays at their bedroom doors.

Daddy knocked and let me know the police officer had
arrived.

I was staring off into space. Auntie Nora told me when we
stare like this, we really aren't looking at air, but something else.
It was a different kind of stare than Sasha's after the assaults.
The way I was staring, Auntie Nora would say, was like I was
looking at some spirit of some kind that our eyes couldn't see
but our souls recognized. Sometimes these spirits can be good,
and maybe it's even the Holy Spirit. I wanted to believe that.

Daddy knocked again, knocking me out of my trancelike
state. He asked if he could come in. I croaked out a yes.

He walked slowly toward me, wearing an expression of un-
certainty, but when near enough, enveloped me in his arms and
rocked me. I leaned my head into the crook of his neck. I so

wanted to cry, to be carried again on his shoulders, to be that child protected in his arms once again.

But no tears came.

Daddy pulled away. He held his hand out for me to take it.

As we walked toward the living room, he murmured Psalm 40:1–2: "I waited patiently for the Lord; and He inclined to me, and heard my cry; He also brought me up out of a horrible pit, out of the miry clay, and set my feet upon a rock, and established my steps."

* * *

Mommy, sitting on a chair facing the police officer, having asked her if she'd like some tea or water, stood up, saying that she would leave us alone.

I looked at the police officer. She was sitting in the middle of the couch, with a notebook resting on her lap and open to a blank page. In one hand, she held a pen.

I sat in the same chair Mommy had just got up from.

I began, not waiting for questions, telling the officer what had happened, every detail I could remember, including how I had met Foxxy on Ning, going to visit her and being led through the bush by her stepbrother, who I was sure was a fake brother. The only detail I left out was Sasha, honouring my promise to her.

I talked and talked for about an hour, surprising myself at how much detail I remembered and how eager I was to get it all out. It was like something inside me was talking for me. Every now and then the police officer would cut in to ask a question, the answers to which she'd write in her notebook. She also wrote down what had been stolen: my Nokia 3310 phone, a red digital camera, a black camera case, and a white battery charger. And my stainless steel ring with two steel grooves.

When I had nothing left inside me to say, the police officer gave me her card and said that I had two options for moving forward: I could make an official report at the St. Ann's Bay police station, or I could make one in the jurisdiction where the assault took place, which would be Spanish Town.

"I have evidence," I said, remembering, when the police officer stood to leave. In my head, I was wondering how I was going to explain Sasha's underwear, without explaining Sasha.

"Bring it to the police station where you report," she said.

I nodded, relieved and confused at the same time, having watched crime dramas on TV. "Don't you want my clothes, shoes?" I then asked. "For DNA ..."

"No. We won't need it."

"Should I go to the hospital?" Now I was really lost, thinking that after I'd gained the courage to report the crime, this woman wasn't taking me seriously.

"You might want to see a doctor tomorrow," she said.

"Can I shower?" I asked, timidly, knowing that after an assault, nurses on American TV shows take DNA swabs.

"Yes."

With my head lowered and in a sinking voice, I thanked her for her time and walked with her to the front door.

"One more thing," she said, stopping and slipping her notebook and pen in her purse and pulling out her car keys.

"Yeah," I piped up quickly, hoping she was going to turn and say, "Can I have your shoes, your clothes, take a DNA swab of your mouth before you shower and wash evidence away ..."

"You seem like you come from a lovely family," she began. My heart started beating fast. I felt heat rising up my back to my neck. "A good church family." I followed her eyes as they moved over the living room, taking in the side tables covered with family and church photographs. "Why don't you leave this lifestyle and return to the church." It wasn't a question.

I felt I had been punched in the solar plexus. For a few seconds I was breathless and in shock. It took every ounce of energy for me to open the door, and thank her again. Even then, I just stood there, staring at the lights of her car as they backed out onto the street, illuminating the bushes of wildflowers.

* * *

Daddy had to shut the front door. He mumbled that he'd heard. *Heard what the police officer had said.* I closed my eyes, feeling the weight of the day crashing down around me, and the thoughts of what I was sure Daddy was going to say next. *That he agreed.*

"I will drive you tomorrow," he said instead. My eyes popped open, startled. I turned and looked into his face, at the dark half moons that sat wedged underneath his eyes, the strain throbbing in the veins of his neck.

"But … but Daddy … you aren't going to say … she's right?"

"I will drive you tomorrow and whenever and wherever you need to go," he reiterated. Mommy now stood beside him.

I saw something in their faces that shocked me: pride. They were hurt and angry that this had happened to me, but they were also proud of what I was doing.

* * *

Alone in the bathroom, I turned on the tap in the shower. I stood waiting for the water to run hot, looking in the mirror at my deadpan eyes until steam covered the image. I then slid off my shirt, jeans, bra, and underpants, pushing them into a pile on the floor with my foot, determined to hand the clothes over to the police along with Sasha's panties.

The shower was hotter than I ever liked it to be. But I didn't care. As the water moved over me, I began to hit myself on the side of the head. Such an idiot, I berated.

I pulled at my hair.

I bit my arms, leaving teeth marks on my skin.

I scratched at my legs, so deeply in a few places I drew blood.

Stop it. Stop it, I finally told myself, breathing hard. This is not your fault.

And I knew that. Did I truly believe that, though?

I heard Rachel's and Annetta's voices in my head — that I was wrong, I was sick.

These are just the words that have been told to you, that you are now telling yourself. Eyes closed, I tilted my head up toward the faucet and filled my mouth with water.

I wanted to drink, but also didn't want any of *their filth* finding its way inside me even more. I filled my mouth with water and then spat. Filled my mouth with water and spat. Then, stepping out onto the bathmat, I grabbed my toothbrush and toothpaste sitting in my cup by the sink. I brushed and brushed my teeth and tongue until my gums were sore.

After that, I reached for the bar of soap and my washing rag.

I stepped back and lathered and washed, lathered and washed, probably ten times, each time watching as the suds circled the drain and then dipped down into the drainage pipe: all my dirt, all his dirt, all Foxxy's fake brother's dirt.

Then the crying came.

And screams, which I tried to muffle by sticking the washing rag in my mouth. I cried and cried, feeling the last of the hot water from the tank leaving, and cool taking its place; a refreshing cool, like the rain that falls on those humid, sunny days in the afternoon.

A sun shower, I thought. And I felt briefly comforted, remembering that sun showers were followed by rainbows.

In my room, changed into my pyjamas, I slipped down to the floor, holding my Bible, which had been a gift from my godmother, Auntie P, a Sister in the Brethren church and a friend of the family, when my parents first moved to St. Ann's Bay.

I found Proverbs 3. I read the entire chapter, saying verses 5 and 6 out loud.

"Trust in the Lord with all your heart and lean not on your own understanding; in all your ways submit to him, and he will make your paths straight."

I then listened to gospel songs.

"The Anchor Holds," by Ray Boltz.

Then: "His Eye Is on the Sparrow."

Followed by: "I Met Jesus at the Crossroads."

And: "Love Lifted Me ..."

I read more Bible passages and listened to more gospel music, until I heard the sounds of morning, pigeons coming to life, cars coming to life, and Mommy boiling water to make her mint tea.

As I crawled into bed for a couple hours of sleep before going to the police station, I prayed once more: Philippians 4:13. "I can do all things through Christ who strengthens me."

CHAPTER TEN

And to the children of our country, regardless of your
gender, our country has sent you a clear message:
Dream with ambition, lead with conviction, and see yourself
in a way that others might not see you, simply because
they've never seen it before.

— *Vice President Kamala Harris*

After that summer of the yellow book, I started at Priory
Primary and Infant School. I went from a class size of about
twenty serious, focused students at a Catholic fee-based school,
to a room full of bubble-gum-chewing, noisy students. I was also
put forward a year, entering Grade 5, because the entire Grade 3
curriculum at my previous school, Columbus Preparatory, was
advanced, Priory staff said.

The Priory students rolled eyes and stole hidden glances of
gloom and doom when certain kids walked past them. This was
my first experience with "exclusion" bullying or silent warfare.

The students who sat at the back of the classroom had soda pop and plantain chips hidden under their desks that they ate during class time. I was a big girl, so while I was a year younger than everyone else in the class, I didn't look it.

For the first few weeks of school, I studied the school dynamics. The most popular girls at Priory seemed to sit near the front of class. I soon learned they did cheerleading and debating and were the class prefects. These girls carried themselves differently than everyone else. They seemed more mature, for one. They were poised, smart, and the heads of every club in the school. These girls had a confidence I had not seen before.

For the first few weeks of school, I met no new friends. The one girl who did talk to me said the kids were whispering that I had to be a snob, since I was coming from a private school. My parents obviously were rich. I knew which kids were talking: the smart ones. I decided one day it was time to start making my entrance into their tight-knit circle. For starters, I got involved in some of the clubs at the school. I wanted friends, so I figured I had to show everyone, especially these girls, I was cool. I didn't have to be part of their "in-group," but I didn't want to be an outsider, either, as it seemed these girls also controlled the cliques. I sat up close behind the girl I was sure was the leader, a tall, slender dark girl named Shanae.

Passive smiles were the most I got until a debate competition. I spoke about capital offences, and whether criminals should face the death penalty. To a standing ovation, I returned to my seat where Shanae congratulated me. During lunch the next day, Shanae's posse of girls plopped themselves down beside me, where I was eating a bagged lunch under a mango tree.

They asked questions about my life and former school, and told me about their lives. Kimmy lived with her grandmother. Her mother was working in the United States, and sent back money in American dollars. Every August, Kimmy would get new school shoes, exercise books, school bags, and clothes that would last most of the school semester. Jessica told me she had a cousin who sold marijuana. He would roll the marijuana into joints and his hands were so rough from grinding. Brianna said her parents were separated and wanting to divorce but in Jamaica divorces took a long time to finalize. Both of Brianna's parents were now seeing other people.

It didn't take long before I was being invited to sit with them at lunch. Nor for them to start divulging their secrets to me, especially of their crushes.

All my girls, Shanae, Jessica, Kimmy, and Brianna, had aspirations to go far in life and be professional women — one a gynecologist and obstetrician, because Jamaica needed more women doctors delivering babies; another an economics professor; another, a lawyer; the fourth, a teacher. I even began referring to them as "my girls."

* * *

Midway through Grade 6, Shanae got a boyfriend. She would show us her hickeys and tell us about the fondling she and her boyfriend had done together on the weekend.

Now her girls, my girls, *me*; we were expected to pick someone, too. A boyfriend, like Shanae, or a crush we would be expected to chase after and eventually land and do things with.

For the first time since my baptism, I was confronted with my feeling more attracted to Shanae than any of the boys my girls would gossip about during lunches.

I prayed for something different; that I would arrive at school and Marlon, who sat behind me in class, or James, who had kissed a girl named Renee at the end of the field, would express an interest in me, and I would like them back. Instead, when Shanae and I would pass and our arms would brush or she would look at me at lunch, I would want it to be *her* that I swooned over. I wanted *her* attention. From head to toe, I tingled when she was near, like I was sailing in some electrical current and every thought led back to her. Afraid she would discover my attraction toward her, I stopped making eye contact, and made excuses to skip our lunches, because of that yellow book saying my liking girls was an infantile stage. I felt such shame over my lusty thoughts that I tried to ignore them, think of something else, just to put the thoughts out of my mind.

But no matter how much distance I tried to put between us, at night, in that time between waking and sleep, I would dream about her liking me back, and what that would feel like.

When she was near, all I could think about was the taste of Annetta's lips and what Shanae's lips would feel like. Or the sensation I had had when, a year earlier, a girl in a different class had watched me go to the bathroom. She was leaning over the stall and when I caught her, I quickly wiped and exited. But before I could leave the bathroom, she had slapped my bottom hard and said, "You have a nice ass."

I liked it. I liked her.

The yellow book promised me, assured me, that I would grow out of liking girls. But if I didn't grow out of it, I'd be a pervert. I wanted someone to talk to about my feelings and how to get rid of them. I wanted to search online to see what I could do to fix myself, but our home computer was set up in the dining room and anyone could see what I was researching. Even when no one was home, I worried Mommy or Daddy would check my search history and I would be caught.

I threw myself more into church and Bible study, and when I couldn't avoid my girls and their talk about the boys they were kissing and touching, I explained to them that being Brethren, young people were expected to wait until marriage to have sex, which included, I told my girls, all the foreplay they were now doing.

"Daddy," I asked him one night, "is it true what Brother Jack says, that we all have a cross to bear?"

"Uh-ha," he said, not really looking up from his reading, which was unusual for him since any talk of the Bible and God usually prompted a sermon-like conversation, where he did more talking at the person than listening. But then again, I had become so religiously fervent, with prayer groups on Tuesdays and youth meetings on Fridays, weekends going with the Sisters and Brothers on outreach, distributing pamphlets to the fishing communities about the Brethren faith, that maybe my endless questions about knowing our path, *my path*, knowing what was right and wrong, had tired even him.

"Daddy," I pressed, "are some people's crosses too heavy to carry? Like are there some sins even *He* will not forgive?"

"Baby," he said, putting down the newspaper and looking at me. "God forgives everyone and everything. You know this. We are all imperfect beings. The fall of mankind, the temptation of Satan, this is what it means to be human. It is in Jesus that we find salvation and forgiveness."

"But what if someone's cross is so big, that even God can't forgive?"

"Angeline, where is this coming from?" He stared at me hard. I thought quickly, recalling a commercial I'd seen on Television Jamaica. Usually the advertisements in between *The Jetsons* and *Paw Paw Bears* were for Chubby sodas or Supligen liquid meal supplement, Milo "the food drink of champions," or Benjamins food colourings, which Mommy used to make ribbon sandwiches. But this one commercial, which was more like a public service announcement, had caught my attention as it was about a girl around my age who was being touched by her mother's boyfriend. The advertisement put out by the National Family Planning Board gave a phone number for girls stuck in situations like this. The narrator called such relationships abuse.

"Like the man in the commercial that was hurting the girl. Would that man be forgiven?" I said to Daddy. It was the only parallel I could come up with, outside of telling him directly I had been reading the yellow book; the yellow book that said that his daughter would turn out to be a pervert because she was more attracted to girls than boys.

Daddy nodded that he remembered the advertisement.

"Will that man be forgiven? Will God forgive him for what he did to her?"

"Well, yes, but only if he repents of his sins," Daddy said. "Angeline, only God and Jesus are perfect. As Colossians says, 'And you, who were dead in your trespasses and the uncircumcision of your flesh, God made alive together with him, having forgiven us all our trespasses, by canceling the record of debt that stood against us with its legal demands. This he set aside, nailing it to the cross.'"

* * *

June came, the last few weeks of school. I would be attending a new school after summer holidays, as Priory ended in Grade 6. If I got strong grades, I'd have a shot at attending St. Hilda's Diocesan High, an all-girls high school with a reputation for strong academics. I'd already written and done well on the GSAT, a two-day-long examination in English, Communication, Social Studies, Science, and Mathematics. Mommy had taught at St. Hilda's early on in her career and it was far away, in Brown's Town, about an hour and a half bus ride each way. None of my girls had St. Hilda's on their list, which was fine with me. I wanted a new beginning. Truth: I respected my girls' drive for success, but outside of that, we had nothing in common.

One Friday, Shanae caught up to me as I was leaving school. She said her parents were out of town; an auntie was minding her but she had a date and would be late. Shanae wanted me to go to her house for an end-of-the-year party. Before I could come up with a reason to say no, she had hooked an arm through mine and was pulling me toward the gate where the others were waiting.

At Shanae's house, I called Mommy, lying, saying I was staying late at school to study, as my girls began changing out of their school uniforms into tight jeans and tank tops. Then they squeezed into the bathroom to share the mirror to put on makeup that they had brought to school and hidden in their bags. I had had no warning, so I had no change of clothes, but even if I had, my non-uniform clothes were church dresses, calf-length skirts, and blouses.

"We're going to a birthday party." Shanae beamed as she pulled clothes from her drawers for me to wear. She was a sapling compared to me and the only things I could fit into were her track pants and a blouse, oversized on her, tight on me.

"Where is the party?" I asked, thinking it was likely a party with my grade.

"It's a party with older people, older teenagers and young adults. A friend of a friend's birthday," Kimmy replied.

From under her bed, Shanae pulled out three beers she boasted that her boyfriend's older brother had bought her. The beers were passed around, the rims soon outlined in the bright red lipsticks they were wearing.

When we were set to leave, the girls put on long skirts and blouses over their party clothes, in case we were seen walking through the neighbourhood by a friend of our parents. The day was bright, with no clouds in the sky. My eyes watered from the light as we headed up the street.

My girls giggled and their walk was more of a skip. Soon the heat of the day, combined with the one sip of alcohol I had taken, made me feel light-headed, like all my worries were lifting away. And I started to feel some excitement.

I'd never been to a real party. The most I'd attended were birthday parties for other kids from Bethlehem Gospel Hall. Those parties involved contemporary gospel music, ice cream, cake, and games like 1, 2, 3 Red Light; Musical Chairs; and Simon Says.

When we turned onto the street of the party, I could hear music. As we stepped up to the house, Shanae cooed that that her favourite song, Diana King's "Shy Guy," was playing. In the yard, I saw large speakers set up in various places.

* * *

Inside the house, my ears rang from the music, the bass of which shook the floor. I couldn't hear my girls when they were talking, saying they wanted to dance or drink or maybe find some food. We ended up communicating mostly through hand gestures.

Kimmy tugged on my shirt, pulling me over to the drink table. I looked at the array of bottles and the cooler filled with beer.

Mommy and Daddy didn't keep alcohol in the house. They only drank at Christmas and then it was a glass of wine. Daddy would have one glass and immediately fall asleep. As Kimmy poured some clear-looking alcohol into a plastic cup, my eyes scanned the table until I recognized one of the bottles: Jamaica's Red Label Wine, which Mommy and Granny Vernice would put in their Christmas puddings. I picked up the bottle. Kimmy urged me to take a sip.

A song came on, the beat of which I loved. Jessica came running up, screaming that it was Mary J. Blige. She stripped off her outer layer of clothing and moved toward the centre of the room where people were dancing. Everyone was gyrating, their hips moving up against each other's. The house itself seemed to have a beat, as everyone moved toward each other and then away.

For a moment, I felt more alive than I ever had, prompting me to drink some more. I slowly started swaying my body to the music.

The more I drank, the hotter I became. I undid the top buttons of my blouse and pushed the waistband of Shanae's track pants down, low riding, to show off my hips, like some of the women in the room had done.

I saw some women dancing with each other, sexy like, and I stared. I found it so attractive to see them, like it was primitive and real to just let go and feel each other's bodies.

I drank more, trying to get up the courage to ask if I could join them.

I spied Shanae on the far side of the room. Our eyes caught and she winked at me. Had I got this all wrong? Did she feel the same about me? With all the alcohol in me, my fears disappeared — about the clobber passages, the yellow book, Annetta and Rachel, the fantasies about Shanae.

I drank some more.

I wanted to dance so bad, dance the way the party was dancing.

I wished I was wearing jeans and a tight top, too. I felt out of place with my clothing.

I drank some more.

And more.

I moved in close to someone, not sure if they were male or female. It could have been Shanae, or maybe just some stranger. At one point I was in the middle of the room, my body just taking over, arms held high over my head, spinning to the music. Dancing, really dancing.

Alive.

Me. I was me. I wasn't hiding. I was free.

Until I felt dizzy.

I grabbed a hold of Kimmy. "I don't feel well," I yelled into her face. I was going to vomit. Kimmy grabbed my hand and pulled me through the crowd, into a darkened bedroom, where she had me lie down on my stomach. Beside me on the floor, she placed a waste paper basket in case I was sick.

And then I passed out.

CHAPTER ELEVEN

God and Nature first made us what we are, and then out of
our own creative genius we make ourselves what we want to
be. Follow always that great law.

Let the sky and God be our limit, and Eternity our
measurement.

— *Marcus Garvey*

June 21, 2009

Daddy never could stop talking about Marcus Garvey, our national hero.

Garvey, the son of a stonemason father, created the Universal Negro Improvement Association and African Communities League, first here, in Jamaica, to empower descendants of enslaved people and to help define an identity for us. He said the descendants of African slaves were the only people in the world who didn't identify with their origins. Garvey was one of the fathers of Pan-Africanism, a cultural and political movement based on those with African roots having common interests and a collective past. Daddy would always remind me: "A people without the knowledge of their history, origin, and culture is like a tree without roots."

In America, Garvey started chapters of his association, and then businesses including the first black press, *Negro World,* which had, for a while, or so Daddy would say, a larger circulation than the *New York Times.* Garvey even launched his own shipping company called the Black Star Line; a symbolic feat, since the shipping experience of the majority of Blacks in North America and the Caribbean involved shackles, imprisoned in the bellies of ships, where many died. The Black Star Line was for Black patrons. They could go back and forth to the islands as first-class citizens. "We are princesses and princes, inheritors of a great land," Daddy liked to say. "Garvey made us believe in ourselves. He gave us a place in this world that wasn't second or even third or fourth class."

The spirit of Garvey burned inside the bellies of us Jamaicans.

We fought. And fought hard. Our politics were bloody, involving people passionately choosing their sides, whether a political party or a gang. Secret deals, exchanges of money and handshakes in the day, murders and attempted assassinations during the night.

But no matter how crushed a Jamaican might be, he or she will rise. Entire communities organized protests closing down roadways — barring traffic and criss-crossing the tarmac with burning tires, boulders, thick tree limbs, sometimes old fridges, and even rusting cars — to demand better roads, or clean water, or to bring attention to a school that was underfunded and falling down. Someone was killed in a hit-and-run accident? There'd be a protest, with a chorus of chanting: "We want justice!"

Daddy may have instilled in me from a young age faith in our Lord and an identity as both a Jamaican and a Black girl, but my island's people showed me how to use my voice as fists. Daddy had that fight, too, so maybe that's why he drove me, as promised, to the Spanish Town Police Station the day following the assaults to file my report. The storm that threatened from the day before was still not coming. I didn't like that. The tempting of things that never came. "Just get it over with," I wanted to shout at the sky.

"You all right?" Daddy asked, after my meeting with Officer Cox of the CIOSCA unit. I had to go in on my own, so Daddy went and met with some clients in the area.

I hummed that I was. And then sighed and admitted I wasn't so sure. I had come to the station with printouts of my text and chat-room conversations with Foxxy, and a detailed, point-by-point document outlining everything that had happened on June 20, leaving out Sasha of course. At one point, when Officer Cox was reading my papers, she sighed and exclaimed, "Not another one!" I felt slapped again, believing at first she was referring to another lesbian filing an assault case, and I readied myself for her advice: "Go back to the church."

But when she started asking me questions about the appearances of the men, I got the sense she was referring to the assault itself. "The men who did this to me, have they done this to other women?" I eventually asked. Did I want to know? Did I want to think that others had been through what Sasha and I had?

Not looking up from my papers, she mumbled, "Uh-huh."

"Mi cyah get dat outta mi head," I told Daddy as he pulled onto the main road that I had taken so many times as a child, on buses, for those Sunday dinners with Granny Vernice.

"What can't you get out of your head?" Daddy asked.

"That there were, *are,* other victims."

"How many?" Daddy asked.

"I doh kno," I replied. Officer Cox said she couldn't tell me. Before we'd headed to Spanish Town, Mommy had booked me an appointment with a gynecologist. I told her that I wasn't alone, but that the other victim wasn't going to see a doctor. The doctor gave me some pills to give to Sasha, probably morning-after pills to stop her from getting pregnant. After I left the doctor's, where the examination included an HIV/AIDS test, Mommy took me to see Mrs. Powell, one of the guidance counsellors at my school. She was also a preacher but in a Pentecostal church. We prayed together for a while. She then took my hands into hers and said, "I hope what happened to you doesn't stop you from finding a good husband. There are good men out there." I was still pretty quiet about being a lesbian. I wasn't public about it and I didn't want to get into any kind of discussion with Mrs. Powell, at least not then, about how same-sex relationships weren't against God and were actually in the Bible. I didn't have the energy to defend myself.

Dr. Nelson, a child psychologist I had met years earlier, had talked to me about a concept called cognitive dissonance. At the time, he felt that inside of me, in my head, I had conflicting attitudes and beliefs. The space in between the conflicting beliefs, which to me felt like a free fall with no end, caused cognitive dissonance. The psychologist believed my way of coping with that downward motion was through compartmentalization. That meant that in order to reconcile these conflicting thoughts and beliefs, I escaped through blocking out one of the beliefs. I can remember his deep, resonant voice — he was a tall man, maybe a foot taller than Daddy — saying, "Parts of your life are too emotionally difficult to accept and hold at the same time. I wonder if when you focus on one area, your coping mechanism is to cut out the other or others. I think there are a number of things inside you that you can't put together."

I craved being able to do that now, to compartmentalize and forget the assault. I had enough of a sense to suspect that I was targeted by Foxxy, Foxxy's fake brother, and the bandana man because I wanted to meet girls. *Corrective rape*: that's the term for it, I had come to learn. These people took it upon themselves to fix me of my wicked ways, believing if I just had sex with a man, I'd be straight.

For a long while, Daddy and I were silent in the car as we drove along the same stretch of highway Sasha and I had taken after the assaults.

When Foxxy's fake brother returned, he'd only had enough money for one of us. "Please let us both on," I had begged the bus driver, a gentle, portly man with greying hair, who I knew from my trips back and forth from St. Ann's Bay to Portmore. He had a wide, kind face and dancing amber eyes. I had felt the eyes of the other passengers staring me down, wanting to know my story, *our story*, my own eyes averting their gaze. Sasha, standing on the road, was pulling further and further into herself.

I had held open my backpack to show the driver I had nothing, nothing except Sasha's bloody underwear, which he saw. Shaking his head, he had looked away, his eyes tearing. The two sun visors above him were flanked with photos of his family, which included daughters my age. "Everything was stolen," I continued, my voice breaking. He looked back at me and waved for us to sit. By the time Sasha had lumbered down the aisle to the vacant seats at the back, she had totally disappeared. She was nothing more than a ghost.

Daddy was talking again. I had zoned out and quickly refocused on his words. He was describing some of the people he sold life insurance to who lived in Spanish Town, including the female police officer who had referred us to Officer Cox. "Good people," he said. "Not what people hear and read about in the newspapers about Spanish Town. Hard-working, Christian folk, trying to make things better. Family people, God loving."

"Daddy," I interrupted, "why is there evil? Why does God allow people to hurt each other?"

"You know this, Angeline. I've talked about this before," he said, and then with a sigh, "Humans were born with free will. We can choose to allow our mind and our impulses to control us, or we can choose to surrender to God and allow God to control us. Evil is not God."

"Daddy," I then said, "can I tell you some things about me, about my life?"

As I talked, I thought back to a folk story Auntie Nora had told me when I was a small child. It went like this:

> Two of the River Mumma's children emerged from the
> water to see a young man, bare chested, with curly hair
> and dimples that, when he smiled at the young women,
> made them blush from his beauty.

"I need to get to the other side," he said to them. "Can you take me?"

The River Mumma had warned her children to not interact with humans. "They will make you fall in love with their words, their reason, until you no longer see the interconnectedness of us all, and become one of them." But the first child, she placed the man on her back. When they reached the other side, she put him down.

The sisters returned to the murky depths of the river. The one sister began to berate the other, until finally the latter spoke up: "I put that man down ages ago. So who of us is still carrying that man?"

The more I laid my story, my burdens, onto Daddy's lap, I realized, the better I felt; that I, like the sister, had been carrying years' worth of baggage.

CHAPTER TWELVE

Cognitive dissonance theory: a theory proposing that people
have a fundamental motivation to maintain consistency
among elements in their cognitive systems. When
inconsistency occurs, people experience an unpleasant
psychological state that motivates them to reduce the
dissonance in a variety of ways.

— APA Dictionary of Psychology

Threes, everything happens in threes, I began. I could tell
Daddy was listening. Really listening.

And three things had happened all in a row, within months
of each other, the first starting with that party with my girls,
like it was the first domino that prompted the others.

After I passed out in that bedroom Kimmy had taken me to,
I woke up, unsure of how much time had passed but knowing it
was at least several hours.

I was on a bed, somewhere, not remembering at first that Kimmy had brought me to the room. That I was at a party. That I had been drinking alcohol.

A light was streaming in through the cracks underneath and around the closed door.

I looked around. The window curtains were open and it was dark out.

I leapt up and off the bed. Fixing my shirt, which had become dishevelled, I ran from the room, pushing through the mass of dancers, until I was out in the street, running at full speed, hearing the music slowly melt into the background, and the quiet of the evening, crickets, and the croaking of a lizard.

I twisted through streets I hardly knew, hoping that my directional skills would lead me to the path that led through the bush to the area where I lived.

I found it, soon enough. And paused before going in. Parents at the church told us kids that sometimes the homeless hung out there. We were warned to never go into this bush alone. But I had no idea of any other way to get home, and I wasn't sure I believed the rumours anyway. The only homeless person I had ever seen in St. Ann's Bay was Mad Man Terry, who hung around the town centre mostly, but occasionally he could be seen at the back corner of the adjoining schools, my old Columbus Preparatory and Marcus Garvey High School, as kids paid him their lunch money to do their math homework. He didn't wear a shirt, even in the rains, and his grey pants were stained and torn. Daddy said he was a genius; so smart that in high school when he learned physics, he kept right on going with the equations, never stopping, not even to bathe. Mad Man Terry was always talking to himself, drumming his fingers as if counting.

I slowed as I approached the wooden bridge that stretched across a gully, the doorway into the bush path. I looked at the sky, knowing that as soon as I entered the bush, the overgrowth of trees would form a covering blocking out any light from the stars. On cloudless nights, Daddy would show my sisters and me the Milky Way. We'd walk down the road until the lampposts ended and, using empty toilet rolls as telescopes, gaze in wonder at the lights in the sky, some brighter than others, some seeming closer than others. Daddy would talk about Heaven lying just beyond and the stars being angels watching over us.

I said a quick prayer, asking God to make sure I made it through to the other side, and crept onto the bridge. My unblinking eyes focused on the darkened dirt path in front of me, the litter that I could see — papers and plastic jugs and bottles. The floorboards creaked. My fears took hold. Mad Man Terry was harmless, I told myself. I'd heard that he even helped the elderly cross the street.

Stepping off the bridge and entering the bush was like stepping into a different world. All the night sounds of the neighbourhood — dogs barking, stray cats meowing, a father calling his kids for dinner — were gone as if sucked up in a vacuum.

The air, too, was still, almost too still.

Then terror really gripped me. I didn't need to be afraid of homeless people. *This is where the duppies live.* While Mommy and Auntie Nora had always talked about duppies being dead people, I'd heard stories about them also being wild animals, and those duppies were the meanest of all. One was a large cow, called the Rolling Calf, which had chains encircling its body and was thought to be the spirit of wicked and dishonest men. Rolling Calf, legend had it, had blazing red eyes that spat fire and its chains dragged behind it causing a loud clanking sound. Auntie Nora said duppies slept underneath cotton trees. I strained my eyes in the deepening darkness to see if there were cotton trees.

I took a deep breath and started running again, the sprawling branches of bushes slapping at my legs and tearing the fabric of Shanae's track pants.

My foot caught on something hard, like a rock or some piece of garbage.

I was flying through the air.

I landed with a thud, somersaulting on the ground, stones digging into my clothes and skin.

When my body came to a stop, I was lying on my back, one leg twisted behind me.

What I thought at that moment was that I shouldn't have drunk so much. I should have done what my girls were doing at the party: meeting boys and making out. That's what girls are supposed to want, right? But because I hadn't, because I wanted Shanae more, because I wanted to dance with girls, my fall was my punishment. Because I had enjoyed myself, for a moment. My church life, my social life, my attraction to girls had all merged, *if just for a moment. A minute. A second.*

In that second, nothing was holding me back.

No bad thoughts.

I was, for that second, just me. And I liked me.

And me was a sick person, a sinner, and I had to be punished.

I don't know how long I was lying there, but after a while, my cries became weak sobs and then the stillness of the bush enveloped me. I listened to my breathing, like the ebb and flow of a tide.

"Shortcut draws blood," I said out loud, as I pulled myself up. "Shortcut draws blood," I repeated as I limped, an ankle sore, perhaps twisted.

Somehow, I told Daddy, I made it safely through the bush, exiting the other side, into my community. I cleaned up for dinner and I was sorry, so sorry, I hadn't told him before what had happened.

* * *

"Daddy, do you remember the big atlas?"

He nodded.

The book was so big, that when I was six, it was still taller than me. The atlas didn't just have maps, but colour photos of the people and different cultures that lived in each country. I was fascinated by anthropology and archaeology. I imagined myself as an adult going on archaeological digs around the world: in Egypt for lost mummies, and the jewels and artifacts the kings and queens took with them to the underworld; to the Tigris-Euphrates Rivers to find the remnants of lost Sumerian culture, or maybe even a four-thousand-year-old skeleton; to Nigeria in search of hundred-year-old masks worn during initiation rituals, or ceremonies, or even rites of passage.

A few weeks after that party, I created an archaeology kit: a shovel, a brush, a magnifying glass, and plastic bags to put my treasures in. I studied maps of St. Ann, current and old, attempting to pinpoint exactly where the Spanish and English colonists might have lived and where I could dig to see if they left anything in the earth.

Another thing that was interesting me was Seville Great House, a former sugar plantation not far from our home. Now part of the Jamaica National Heritage Trust as a museum, it had artifacts from the slaves that had worked the sugar cane fields on display — like the ceramic bowls and enamel mugs used by enslaved Africans as far back as the early 1700s, and dolls carved out of wood or made from metal, resembling the masks and dolls used in ceremonies in West Africa. The museum even displayed torture items used by slave masters — whips, chains, and the handcuffs worn while stolen Africans were transported to the islands.

Every August, the great house on the plantation would put on a festival. Guests could tour the sugar mill. Junkanoo dancing, a form of freedom for slaves, would be featured. Junkanoo dancers would come toward me, take my hand, and have me do a few moves with them. Drawing on the intricate carvings and paintings of various African tribes, masks would be designed in elaborate representations of spirits and wanderers. The few holidays slaves had — around Christmas Eve and Boxing Day — was when Junkanoo dancing in Jamaica was celebrated, and several of the islands in the Caribbean hold Junkanoo parades in and around the Christmas season.

What if I could find a mask worn by a slave from the 1800s?

That summer the weather was hot, sticky, and sunny, no hurricanes this season, so my family and I spent a lot of Saturdays at Priory Beach. Mommy would pack a picnic of sandwiches she filled with Tastee Cheese. She'd dye the cheese different colours — reds, yellows, and blues — to make ribbon sandwiches, and cut them into shapes like triangles or tiny squares. Daddy would pick up some patties on the way. For a while, we would all play in the water, cooling ourselves off, throwing a ball around or playing tag. After, Daddy would fall asleep on a towel laid out on the sand, and Mommy would read a book lying beside him. Latoya and Toni would spread out their plastic shovels and pails, and build monster-sized sandcastles, which they'd adorn with seashells.

On this one Saturday, I meandered off with my archaeology kit, which I carried in a backpack. I dug in a few places, but found nothing but crabs. It was so hot, I soon was perspiring and breathing heavily. I was about eighty metres away from Mommy and Daddy and my sisters, when I sat down with a sigh and dug my toes into the sand. I was pouting, covering my legs with sand, so I didn't see them approach: two older boys, maybe eighteen or nineteen years old.

"Hey, what are you up to?" one asked.

"You have a pretty smile," the other said. (I wasn't smiling.) "We're going over to the other side of the beach. Do you want to come with us?"

"No, I'm okay. I am fine here."

"Come on. You look pretty. We like how you look."

"Go away," I finally said. "My parents are over there." I waved in the direction of Mommy and Daddy. I quickly glanced around the beach. There was no one in sight. It was late afternoon. The day people had gone home, and the evening crowd of young people and families having beach barbecues had not arrived yet.

They moved so fast, those boys. Each reached into the sand and grabbed ahold of one of my ankles. They started dragging me along the beach, toward some bushes.

I screamed. I yelled for Mommy, for Daddy, for my sisters to hear, but the wind was blowing in the opposite direction. My voice, like a kite, was jousting up and down and moving away.

I kicked real hard, harder than I ever have, grateful in that moment for cheerleading, for I knew how to kick high, and I angled the ball of my foot so it punched one of the men in the groin. He bent over in pain, loosening his grip on my foot. Instinctively, I pulled it away, and swivelled my body to kick the other man hard in his face, this time with the flat front of my foot, chaffing his cheek. I then kicked him hard on his chin.

With both feet freed, I scrambled up and ran toward my sisters, trampling over their sandcastle, slowing my pace just enough to grab hold of each of their arms. I didn't stop until we all fell down on the sand beside Mommy and Daddy, panting for air.

When I looked over, the men were gone. *Gone.* Everything happened with such lightning speed, I wondered briefly if it had all been a mirage.

* * *

I was no longer in touch with my girls that summer. We had graduated from Priory Primary and Infant School on a hot, windless day, the ceremony held inside a church. All of us were suffocating from the heat. The church was so crowded, people spilled out into the street and garden, unable to see their child get their certificate or an award. After the ceremony, my girls and I hugged and I said my goodbyes. We were all going to different schools in September.

But after the incident on the beach, I wanted my girls — their wisdom, their street smarts. I wanted to ask them why those men did this to me? Was this happening to them, too? What should I do?

The recipient of my queries ended up being our babysitter, Amoy; a tall, lanky twentysomething woman, soft spoken, with creamy skin. She wore fuchsia blush, matching lipstick, and baby-blue eyeshadow. Most women in my church didn't wear makeup and, unlike my girls, I wasn't interested in it. But I was fascinated by Amoy; her elegant walk, her long limbs, the way she tucked her skirt underneath her when she sat down.

"What is it like to be with a boy?" I asked her one day. Toni and Latoya were in their room practising a play they were to perform at church.

"Ahhh." She smiled, then laughed, as her eyes moved up and down my body, making me feel uncomfortable. "I guess you're about the age when your body starts wanting a boyfriend. Do you have a crush on someone?"

I shrugged.

"Being in love is magical," she said, closing her eyes and hugging herself. "Being in love is our way of knowing how much God loves us. When we love someone else, it's how God loves us."

I paused, thinking real hard what this love felt like. Like the trust I had for Mommy and Daddy? No, I thought. More like the way I felt about Shanae, the tingling when she was near. How when I would wake in the mornings it was as if she was there. Her energy, you know? That, I thought, that is what love has to be. "But what about being with a boy you don't like?" I asked next. "When you don't want to be with him? When it doesn't feel like love?"

Amoy became defensive. "Has someone touched you?" she demanded.

"No." I shook my head. "No," I repeated.

I wanted to tell Amoy about the party and the two men on the beach. I wanted to confide in Amoy that I liked, no loved, a girl, not a boy. I wanted to ask if God was punishing me because something was wrong with me. But the words were stuck deep down in my stomach and would not come out.

"Has something happened to someone you know?" she asked next. "Did some boy touch a friend of yours?"

Again I shook my head.

Amoy dove in then, talking about the men that just take advantage, who force themselves on women and girls. "I've been hit on too many times, I lost count," she said. "But you have to almost play a game. The more you protest 'no,' the more they become aggressive, like somehow getting angry at their advances fuels them on."

On that day, I learned from Amoy the word *rape* and what it meant.

I recalled that public service advertisement about the girl being abused by her mother's boyfriend. Now it all made sense.

Now I understood, and I vowed to take precautions, like always being with someone when in a new place.

Another time, Amoy picked me up to take me to church for a youth meeting. We headed out onto the street and waited for a taxi to drive by. En route, Amoy had us stop at a neighbour's, Mr. Gordon's, house. Amoy said she had to pick something up from him. I went into the house with her, sat on a couch, television on, and was given some banana chips to eat. Amoy and Mr. Gordon went into a back room. A few minutes later, I heard groans and moans. These were, I was sure, sex sounds. And Mr. Gordon, I also knew, was a married man.

Whatever clarity I had gotten from my previous conversation with Amoy was now clouded with confusion and more questions. Why was it wrong for me to love a girl, but not wrong for Amoy to love a man who loved another woman?

* * *

The third thing that happened that summer was I got my period. And with it, the fantasies of girls crashed into me like a tidal wave. I couldn't stop the images in my head, which aroused my body with pleasant sensations. These thoughts made me hot, my cheeks flushed, and I wanted to touch myself.

My drive, my natural impulse to be with a girl who wanted to be with me, intensified.

I'd move to naturally do what I felt my body was calling for, then remember that yellow book and its warning that self pleasure was not the ideal type of sexual activity.

With the changes in my body and with my emotions and fantasies curdling and bubbling up around me, the guilt punctured and hammered at me. I'd ball up a section of my clothes and push it into my mouth and just scream. I'd then pray and pray, until the urges had passed and the narrative I was telling myself that I was a sinner had tapered to a whisper. I'd listen to Love 101, while reading from the Bible.

"Have I not commanded you? Be strong and courageous. Do not be afraid; do not be discouraged, for the Lord your God will be with you wherever you go." Joshua 1:9.

I may have felt relaxed in the sanctuary of my church life, my life with God, but these moments became fleeting. There was always an undertow pulling me back toward my body, the now, the realness, and wanting to touch and be touched by girls.

At church one Sunday near the end of summer holidays, the congregation singing the hymn "Joyful, Joyful, We Adore Thee," I began to swoon. Our church was single storey, made of concrete, painted the colour of curdled milk. There were about twelve rows of wooden benches, with an aisle in between. An iron grill made a case that held the speaker box. When we sang, the amplified music and our voices moving together made me think that this was how the angels welcomed us into Heaven.

But on this day, I didn't feel a part of the chorus. And on this day the speaker box was resting on the floor for some reason.

"You wrang, Angeline," I heard Annetta say in my head.

I sang louder, trying to block her out.

"Hearts unfold like flow'rs before You / Op'ning to the sun above …"

I heard Annetta say next, "It wrang what you did." It wrang. Yuh wrang. You are wrong!

Like when I went to that party, there was a throbbing of the bass coming up through the floorboards.

I closed my eyes.

"Melt the clouds of sin and sadness / Drive the dark of doubt away …"

I felt the hands of the men around my feet, pulling me along the beach.

I became dizzy.

Swaying.

I closed my eyes and saw myself weaving in and out of clouds and mist. Mommy told me afterward, on the way to the hospital, that my body had shook and trembled. I'd had a seizure, she explained.

At the hospital, I asked her if what happened to me was like the time this one lady in church started speaking in tongues. It was as if something had come in and taken over her body. The lady had said it was the Holy Ghost. I was afraid of that, because our church didn't like extreme shows of ecstasy or acts like possession. The Brethren were reserved people, someone had said to me after, and the lady was indirectly shamed into leaving until she could contain herself.

"No," Mommy replied in a soft voice, stroking my forehead. "You're sick with something. The doctors don't know yet."

Dr. Nelson, the hospital psychologist, sat with me for about an hour, asking all sorts of questions. I wanted to tell him about myself, about what I was sure now was an attempted rape at the beach, about my confusion — why couldn't I like girls and also love God? But the words were stuck deep down in some cellar.

Dr. Nelson told Mommy and Daddy he thought I was having a mental breakdown, due to stress. But my family doctor, who took over my care when I was released from the hospital, told Mommy and Daddy that he disagreed. "At Angeline's young age, and with her stable family, good marks, and the church, there is nothing to cause her stress," he said. "Let's keep an eye on things. If Angeline passes out again like that, we'll send her for more medical tests in Kingston."

CHAPTER THIRTEEN

Daniel answered, "Long live the king! My God sent his angel
to shut the lions' mouths so that they would not hurt me,
for I have been found innocent in his sight. And I have not
wronged you, Your Majesty."

— Daniel 6, Daniel in the Lion's Den

Late July 2009

Officer Cox called me on the new cellphone Mommy had picked
up for me, saying the police had raided a house. From the police
report I had filed that included a list of my stolen items, Officer
Cox believed they'd found my things. She asked if I could come
to the station, and bring my stolen cellphone's original box so
they could match up the IMEI numbers, a type of serial number
connected only to my phone.

I was shocked about the timing: namely, it was so fast. Police
in Jamaica, but especially Spanish Town, had a reputation of being

corrupt and slow, if they did anything at all. Sasha had said to me when we made it safely back to the main road, a few minutes away from where the whole nightmare with Foxxy's fake brother began, "What if we're being followed right now? What if the attackers see us go to the police station and then after, track us down and kill us? Or what if a police officer tells them? No way I go to the police. Not here. Not nowhere on this island." Even if there was no corruption, the radio news and newspapers were constantly reporting on how there were too many crimes, and too few police.

The police station was cool, a large industrial fan forcing air circulation. I gave my name at the front desk and said I was there to meet Officer Cox. As I was being escorted to the witness waiting room, I heard the front desk sergeant say to another officer: "She's the first person with evidence to come forward. She goin' ID him." I wasn't sure if they were talking about me or someone else.

In a small windowless room lit by fluorescent bulbs, the walls painted white and black, with white and grey terrazzo tiles, I waited impatiently, tapping a foot, my mind churning.

What if I have to see the men who attacked me?

Are they even here? Have they been arrested?

I stood when Officer Cox entered the room and asked how I was doing.

I mumbled, "Okay." After a few minutes of small talk, she laid out on the table my red digital camera, my sterling silver ring, about three thousand in Jamaican dollars, and my cellphone, each wrapped in its own clear plastic bag, with evidence numbers written in black Sharpie on the front.

Officer Cox took a seat across from me, the chair's metal legs scratching the floor, while I ploughed through my backpack of school papers and books for the cellphone box. The numbers matched. I asked if I could look at my camera. Keeping it in its plastic bag, I pushed the "on" button. All my photos, including the one I took of Sasha when we'd started out *that day*, were still there. My eyes puddled and I looked up at the ceiling to stop myself from crying. Officer Cox, seeming to understand, said to take a few minutes for myself.

"Do I have to ID the man, the men, today?" I eventually mumbled, looking at her through liquid eyes.

"No," she said in a soothing voice. "May I ask you a question?"

I nodded yes.

"Are you a lesbian?"

I moved my head in a slow nod, my eyes glued to hers, unblinking, wondering why … why now would she ask? The room fell silent. I heard the whir of the air conditioning. The chatter of muffled voices outside in the hallway. I waited, breath held in, for her to tell me they were dropping the case because of my liking girls.

"Thank you," she whispered instead, reaching out and squeezing my hand. Her hand was warm and clammy. "You're very brave. When we have apprehended the person in question, we will call you into the station then. Are you okay with ID'ing him?"

"You mean you haven't arrested them?" I asked, startled.

"No. The suspect wasn't home. But we're searching for him."

"You are only looking for one of them?"

"We think we know who the other man is, too. We're looking for both of them."

"Why …" I started then stopped.

"Why what?"

"Why are you moving so quickly, so fast? I mean, I thought investigations took a long time, years even."

"It's an ongoing investigation, and because of that, I can't tell you anything at this time."

I nodded to show I understood. Still fixated on Officer Cox's eyes, I studied her, wishing I had the gift of others I had met over the years who seemed to be able to look into someone's eyes and just know the thoughts, emotions, and words that were going unsaid. The only read I could get was that Officer Cox cared.

* * *

I stepped back out into the humid air, feeling the warmth of the sun bathing my chilled bare arms and heating up my dark shirt.

Daddy was still at his appointments, which I'd suspected beforehand would go longer than my time needed at the station, so I walked to get a Bigga Kola Champagne Soda.

Earlier that week, I had called the only other person I knew who lived in Spanish Town. She was a lesbian, too, and we'd met on Rainbow Vibes and became friends. Her name was Anita. I told her everything I could about Foxxy, being lured to a secluded place, and the attack. When I was done, she was silent for a while. She then said she'd heard my story before. My assault, right down to Foxxy befriending another girl online. Before we hung up, Anita told me she'd make a call to the other victim. A few days later, Anita texted me the number for Catherine.

After I got my drink, I found a bench that gave me a view of the police station so I could see Daddy drive up. I sipped slowly, closing my eyes, letting the cool liquid fall slowly, and letting the sun drench me in its light, my mind drifting away into nothingness. I listened to the soft wind rustling the leaves in a Blue Mahoe tree.

Often when I closed my eyes, I'd see Sasha in my mind, being assaulted all over again first by Foxxy's fake brother and then by the man in the bandana. My standing there, unable to do anything, helpless, hopeless, crying, and praying. A few times I'd wake in the night, haunted by these images and crushing guilt, heart racing, my pyjamas soaked from sweat and my hands shaking. I would sob then, remembering, *remembering*, she had come as my friend. She could have said no. She had come with me to meet Foxxy, so I would have a companion and be safe. On one of these nights, I thought of the Bible story about the Medes and Persians who issued a law that prayer could only be directed toward King Darius. This law was how they wanted to entrap Daniel, who was a well-trusted confidant of the king and thought to be incorruptible. Daniel, as expected, continued to pray to God and was thrown into the lion's den as punishment. But unlike Daniel, Sasha didn't have a guardian angel protecting her, aiding her in her escape. What happened to her was my fault. As Corinthians says, "Do not be deceived: Bad company ruins good morals." What had I done ... done to Sasha?

"Dear God," I began praying softly, "please give me the strength and courage to continue to provide comfort to Sasha." What comfort I could, that was. After I had given Sasha the medication from the doctor, I started pulling away from her. Ashamed to talk to her, feeling guilty for what happened to her. It was too painful.

When I was done praying, I called Catherine. Her voice came on the line, deep and throaty. I introduced myself.

"I know who you are," she said. "Sorry bout wah happen to you."

"Anita said …" My voice drifted. How do you ask someone: "Can you tell me about your assault? Can you tell me how you were raped?"

"That it happened to me, too?" she picked up.

"Yes," I exhaled.

"At night. Foxxy and I planned to meet up before a party," she said. "But she never showed. Just her broda."

"You met on Rainbow Vibes?"

"Yeah. Messaged for months. At first our conversations were formal. She'd ask about my day. She seemed really interested in how I lived. Not many people around me care about what I do, about my feelings, you know. Not many people around me seem to even see me. She did. Or seemed to. Then it changed. Her messages and mine to her became more sexy."

"Same with me," I said, shaking my head.

She sighed. "I know two other girls it happened to as well. One was young, like you, thinking she was meeting another girl like her."

I gasped. "Did you ever … did the others … did anyone go to the police?" I stopped and started, my voice both pleading and excited. I needed these women and girls to stand up with me. Then I wouldn't feel so alone.

"None of us went to the police."

I felt like I was falling.

"I work in a grocery store. I live and work in Spanish Town," she said. "I have a young son. I can't have people knowing …"

"Knowing you're gay?"

"Yeah."

"Thank you for sharing what you have," I finally said, trying to be patient, but inside I was angry, hurt, lost.

She ended our conversation saying she had to keep safe and live a false life. Her voice was full of longing, dragging, as if wanting me to understand and agree; as if she was trying to convince herself she agreed.

The problem was, I did understand. I understood far too well.

* * *

Back at home, a few days before August holidays, Emancipation Day and Jamaica's Independence Day, my phone lit up with text messages from Foxxy.

> Would you want to try meeting again?
> I still want to kiss you.
> Hey you. How've you been? I miss talking to you. I wish I could see you.
> I'm sorry I wasn't at the house. Trus mi, if I coulda do dat day ova, I would.

Who are you? I wanted to write back. Tell me the truth. I picked up my phone, set to call her. "Are you even real?" I wanted to yell. "Are you Foxxy or that fake-brother of yours, pretending to be Foxxy, or the man in the bandana? Who was the woman I spoke to on the phone? Whose picture was online? Someone you paid to pretend ... pretend to like me?"

Instead, I wrote simply:

Thanks

She wrote back immediately:

Yuh wah try meet again?

Yuh tek mi fi idiot? Maybe Sasha was right: these men had an insider at the police station. These men knew I had reported what they had done to me. The men, the assaulters, knew the police were circling them. They had to. One of their homes had been raided.

I became paranoid, moving through the house, shutting and locking any open window, thinking I was being watched. I looked out the front door, glancing up and down the garden, then I skirted down the driveway to the street, straining to see if there was a car I didn't recognize, parked, with passengers inside with binoculars? Anything that seemed out of the ordinary. I scrolled up on all my messages with Foxxy, seeing if I had ever written where I lived. I hadn't even mentioned St. Ann's Bay. *But then if they do have an insider with the police, they'd know where my home was.*

I felt I had no choice but to play along, at least until I could ask Officer Cox what I should do.

Sure. Where do you want to meet?

In my head, I am counting five of us, women of various ages. If I was the only one coming forward, I told myself, I had to stay rational and alert to have any chance of sending these people to jail. If they didn't have a police informant in their pocket, I couldn't let on to Foxxy, or her fake brother, or the man in the bandana that they were being hunted, or that I was involved, so as to give the police a better chance of trapping them. For sure, I was never going to actually attempt to get together with Foxxy.

CHAPTER FOURTEEN

Blessed are the poor in spirit, for theirs is the kingdom
of heaven.
Blessed are they who mourn, for they shall be
comforted.
Blessed are the meek, for they shall inherit the earth.
Blessed are they who hunger and thirst for
righteousness, for they shall be satisfied.
Blessed are the merciful, for they shall obtain mercy.
Blessed are the pure of heart, for they shall see God.
Blessed are the peacemakers, for they shall be called
children of God.
Blessed are they who are persecuted for the sake of
righteousness, for theirs is the kingdom of heaven.

— *Beatitudes, Matthew 5:3-10*

I started First Form, high school in Jamaica, at St. Hilda's.
I joined the only club that interested me: debate.

For the first few weeks of class, we students were mostly quiet, focused on the teacher, especially those who sat near the front, like I did, waiting, I guess, to form our alliances and friendships. A girl named Amelia, also in debate, eventually invited me to have lunch with her.

Two other girls joined us, and for weeks, when we ate, we would get into long, deep intellectual talks, mostly with Amelia leading. Amelia and the other girls, also in debate, soon started meeting after school as well, in the dining hall. Amelia said she wanted the debate team to make it to the parish championships, and we needed as much practice as we all could get. During our practice debates, the other two girls and I tried to interject, but when Amelia got talking she took over. On the topic of Marcus Garvey, she asked *was he a revolutionary or a madman* ... ending her argument by saying there was a fine line between greatness and insanity.

I didn't know a lot of the words Amelia was using, so while she kept on with her arguments, I would quickly flip through my pocket dictionary, collecting an army of new words to use in my own debates.

One time, outside under the almond tree, Amelia, pacing as the rest of us sat cross-legged on the ground, debated on the subject of the Maroons — who in Jamaica were predominantly former enslaved Africans who escaped the Spanish plantations and joined with some of the surviving Tainos creating settlements in the mountains.

Amelia focused her debate on asking whether the Maroons were freedom fighters, or whether they were pacifists that refused to take up arms against the British and defend the hundreds of thousands of enslaved Africans brought to Jamaica over several hundred years.

I couldn't keep up with her. She was an encyclopedia.

When she talked about religion, I took notes, in part because I was taking religious education, which involved learning about other faiths.

"I think Jesus could have been a Buddhist," she said, not in a loud voice, but not soft, either.

I coughed from surprise.

Amelia looked over and smiled at me, a weak smile, nothing much more than a curl of the upper lip, but enough to draw me into her even more. It was the first time I actually thought she was paying real attention to me.

"Should the scriptures be taken verbatim, or as stories, reflecting the society during the time of writing?" she continued. I was speechless. I had never heard anyone challenge the Bible. But she didn't seem afraid, just cautious, knowing if a teacher in our Anglican-founded school overheard she might be reprimanded or even sent to detention. "Like if Jesus was alive today, born in Jamaica, he'd be a Black man with locs, who played a funde or kete drum or bamboo scraper. I wouldn't surprise if him would a smoke weed, too. Maybe what we need to take away from the scriptures is just the meaning ... not the literal facts." When she lectured, she flung her hands around like a band master.

"Look at Deuteronomy. It says" — Amelia pulled out her Bible — "'If a man meets a virgin who is not betrothed, and seizes her and lies with her, and they are found, then the man who lay with her shall give to the father of the young woman fifty shekels of silver, and she shall be his wife, because he has violated her. He may not divorce her all his days.'

"Nuh rape dat? So if she get rape she haffi marry di rapist? How dat can mek sense?" Amelia paused. "And look at the contradictions right here," she picked up. "Matthew says, 'whoever divorces his wife, except for sexual immorality, and marries another, commits adultery' ... whereas Deuteronomy says, 'When a man hath taken a wife, and married her, and it come to pass that she find no favour in his eyes, because he hath found some uncleanness in her: then let him write her a bill of divorcement, and give *it* in her hand, and send her out of his house.'

"First off, one place says divorce is okay, another not okay. And everything is from the perspective of the man, like women are just possessions. I know of no Jamaican woman who does not have a voice, is not strong, is not striving to be an equal."

When I got home I looked up Buddhism on the computer, eventually coming away thinking, *Huh, Amelia may not be far off.* Matthew's Beatitudes sounded an awful lot like Buddhism's Eightfold Path, and when I read about traits of the Buddha, I couldn't help but think he'd dedicated his life to living a certain way that sounded a lot like Jesus, too.

I wanted to get to school to talk to Amelia, to get her all on my own and have her share with me more of her vast knowledge. I felt like she had opened inside of me a treasure box, and I hoped she'd go inside with me and pick through every item one by one.

On the bus, I couldn't stop thinking of Amelia and how alive she made me feel. It was like in her conversations, she was sending me secret codes.

I understand you.

I am like you.

I wondered if I was sending her telepathic codes right back: "Let's hang out together." Maybe there will be a time when we don't even need language? I mused. When we can just feel and read each other's thoughts and emotions.

Amelia only showed up for P.E. class — a sweaty afternoon period of netball. When I saw her, my hands grew clammy, and my mouth dry. I was extremely conscious of how I smelled — did I give off a scent of sweetness or musk, or grease and heavy body smells? I stood off to the side as she passed the ball to the goal shooter.

After the game, my class headed to the change room. I was slipping back into my school uniform — a solid lavender tunic, worn over a lavender plaid button-down blouse. I kept glancing over at Amelia, whose back was to me. Then she turned and looked right at me, as if she knew I was staring. She started coming toward me. I braced myself, thinking, *This is it, the moment we come together.*

Infinity.

My pulse raced and I realized I couldn't move. As she neared, I looked closely into her dark brown eyes, round, doughy, like the fried doughnut holes Mommy and I would make.

She stopped right in front of me with a huff. "Yuh ' ave a ting fi mi?" she asked, stomping a foot.

I swallowed hard. Amelia, I should also say, had a loud voice.

I dug down deep, mustering up the courage to push the words out, figuring there was a fifty-fifty chance she might become my first girlfriend if she didn't see my fear, which I was sure I was spraying out like a rain shower, and find cowardliness a turnoff.

"So what if I do," I said as confidently as I could. I was sure I sounded like a coughing lizard, but I pulled my shoulders back and stood tall, hopeful she liked the wobble in my voice, saw my nervousness as a sweet vulnerability.

"You a lesbian?" she asked, her lips pursed, her head slightly tilted. Her obvious disdain for me triggered memories of Annetta and Rachel.

I felt like an animal, trapped in front of a moving car, about to be roadkill. I was frozen. I couldn't move. I couldn't speak. I couldn't breathe.

"Stay far from mi!" she snapped.

She turned on the balls of her bare feet and stomped her way back to where she had been changing.

Feeling both invisible and naked in front of everyone, I wobbled to finish changing. I was the last one to leave the room. On trembling, rubber legs, I made my way to the nurse's office. I saw the bed, empty, a white paper sheet pulled tight across it. I collapsed on my stomach, my legs dangling over the side, my entire body contorting and moving as if by its own will.

Disappeared.

I disappeared.

Another seizure.

* * *

Over the next few months, Daddy drove me back and forth to Kingston for hospital tests. Doctors ruled out epilepsy, multiple sclerosis, and all the other neurological illnesses they could.

I'd had no stroke, the brain scans confirmed.

And my heart was beating just fine.

I didn't have a cancerous cyst in my head causing me to black out. I was simply having seizures the various doctors could not explain.

In the months that followed, I stayed home from school but kept up with my work from home. I wasn't sure if I was even there. I felt like I was a spectator, watching my life, the footage of a grainy, crackling black-and-white film.

No colours.

No light.

Just hanging on.

Surfacing.

Drowning.

Treading water.

I was sure I was dying.

I was sure I had only a short time left on earth.

* * *

Life takes on a different sense of meaning, I thought one day, when you realize that tomorrow may be your last. My prayers became less about the words and more about my connection with God and Jesus. I wanted to spend every minute possible with Mommy and Daddy, hearing them talk about their lives before me, their dreams, how they met, how they found God. I wondered if they would be okay after I died, or would they spend months if not years mourning me.

When alone in the house, I would spend hours in prayer, often losing track of entire blocks of time. And the more I prayed, the more I laid my sins and my guilt and my shame at God's and Jesus's feet, I realized that Amelia was right: God was kind and merciful. He didn't judge. Almost like a revelation, I recognized that God was one thing and one thing only: LOVE. He was perfect and my imperfections were doubting the impulses and love He had given me and that, by extension, I could give others.

Amelia had, in her refusal of my love, given me a great gift in return.

Daddy told me when I was little that God works in mysterious ways. The answers we seek, His guidance, are always given, even in hardship. But you need to be able to see, to hear, to feel the answers.

Trust. Surrender. Let go.

I repeated these words, over and over, until it was like they were stuck in my head. Every time I closed my eyes, it was like these words were visible on the inside of my eyelids. They were a part of everything I did.

I came to realize that I was denying my full potential. I was part of God. The Holy Spirit was in me. I was made in God's image. Even as a lesbian, God knew me as I was being formed in my mother's womb. When God looked at creation and said it was good, that also included me. The grace and salvation that Jesus brought by dying on the Cross would heal my sins. And no, my sin wasn't liking girls but rather the things I did that harmed and hurt others and hurt myself.

As John 1 says: "Beloved, now we are children of God; and it has not yet been revealed what we shall be, but we know that when He is revealed, we shall be like Him, for we shall see Him as He is."

* * *

I woke up one day a few months before the start of summer holidays and announced to Mommy and Daddy that I was ready to try going back to school on a regular basis. I hadn't had a seizure since the start of the new year. What I didn't tell them was that since I was dying, I no longer cared what Amelia or Rachel or Annetta thought of me. I no longer feared who I was. And if possible, I had prayed to God, before I died I wanted to kiss a girl, to love a girl, and to receive love from a girl, figuring that there had to be someone else like me in a school of hundreds of girls.

I sat at the back of the classroom as far away from Amelia as I could. I may not have cared what she *had* said, but I wasn't a fool, either, to walk right back into the lion's den.

And that's when I started to see an intimacy between the other girls that surprised me and made me feel welcome. These girls, tucked in the back, would sit on each other's laps, brush each other's hair, tickle each other's necks. Sometimes after lunch, I would find them with their legs stretched out over each other's, giggling — almost, I thought, flirting. The more I got to know and be accepted among these girls, the more I discovered that several had boyfriends. But nonetheless they did not feel threatened by expressing their fondness for each other, too, like the girls I'd seen dancing at that party before I blacked out. There wasn't one outward characteristic that defined this group, not like other cliques, not like my girls. Some were heavy, like me, tough on the outside, soft like seafoam on the inside; some were the other way round; others were dainty and fragile inside and out, it seemed. A few came from well-off families; a few were being raised by grandparents or other relatives while their parents worked in America.

I became close, near the end of that year, with Sasha, who sidled up beside me in the dining room one lunch and, after we got to know each other well enough, told me she was angry at Amelia for what she had said to me in P.E. class. "She's a smartass, you know. She wears a shell, like a turtle shell." Sasha laughed. "Like she's hiding something inside her, if you know what I mean." She winked then. In my hiatus at home, I had half suspected Amelia liked girls, too, and was ashamed. Maybe her way of coping was to publicly humiliate me instead. If I had thought Amelia was sending me secret codes, Sasha was at least speaking my language.

Sasha and I became so comfortable with each other that we even shared our mutual crush on our integrated science teacher, Miss Brown. Squat, with warm brown skin like milk chocolate and a straight shiny weave that curled slightly under her chin, Miss Brown would walk around the room, her large bottom and wide hips sashaying like a dance. Sasha and I would stare at her bottom, both of us liking it.

Sasha and the girls at the back spoke about Obeah, a spiritual practice that had its origins with our African ancestors and which was practised by slaves even after the British outlawed the practice in 1898. Obeah involves connecting with ancestors and spirits and doing healing rituals, which the English felt were spells and witchcraft. Sasha told me that if I saw a house with a long bamboo pole and coloured flags in the front yard, the owner likely practised Obeah. St. Thomas, especially, was said to have a lot of Obeah practitioners who could perform a ritual for almost anything I wanted. Love. Money. A curing of illness. To lift a string of bad luck or to remove a bully or an abusive person from my life. "Bring the practitioner a bullfrog and a padlock for a ritual," Sasha explained. "That's all you have to do." I loved learning about the different religions and spiritual practices of our island. I was fascinated that there was so much more that existed beyond Christianity. And maybe in these other practices I could heal whatever was wrong with me and I would no longer be dying, I thought.

And sure enough, I did escape death. A few weeks after I started to learn about Obeah and after a CT scan at an appointment in Kingston, a doctor reiterated what I had been told by other medical staff. While he didn't know what was wrong with me, I was most certainly not dying.

* * *

"I'm gay," Sasha announced, the two of us in a back corner at the St. Ann's Bay Library, studying for exams. Her words came from out of nowhere, startling me. I became stone still. "I'm gay. I just thought you should know. I hope you don't hate me now," she stammered, her voice fading. "I hope you will still be my friend?"

I still didn't move. Didn't say anything.

"Do you know what it means to be gay?" she then asked, thinking this was the reason I had turned into a concrete statue, like Lot's wife becoming a pillar of salt. "It means I like girls. I want to be with a girl."

I finally swerved my head and looked at Sasha. Even more slowly, I leaned toward her.

When I was real close, I whispered, "I'm gay, too."

Shock took hold of me again. This time, it was from the relief that I felt as those words spilled out of me. I had to say them over and over and over.

"I am gay, too. I am gay, too."

I am gay.

Tears came to my eyes.

Sasha took my hand. "A secret shared is no longer a burden," she said, with a warm smile.

Like a giant exhale, my secret, shared with only God, was now out.

I was out.

The entire weekend that followed, Sasha and I met at the library, trying to study, but in the quiet of a long table located in the back, she and I talked in hushed voices about our lives, our gay lives, and the shame and fear that we both lived with.

We concluded that we didn't have the attraction toward each other that we had for, say, Miss Brown, but in tandem we forged a relationship of support for each other, sharing everything we knew, including the revelations I had had over the course of the year that God is love. And that if we come just from that place, no matter who the object of our love is, we are a vessel of God. Conformity, judgment, hate, guilt, and shame, I told her, was not God.

Sasha agreed.

I was finally not alone.

CHAPTER FIFTEEN

Section 76. Unnatural Offences. Whosoever shall
be convicted of the abominable crime of buggery,
committed either with mankind or with any animal, shall
be liable to be imprisoned and kept to hard labour for a
term not exceeding ten years.

— *The Offences Against the Person Act (OAPA), Jamaica*

Mid-August 2009

The Spanish Town police had a suspect in custody, and Officer
Cox asked me to come to the police station and do an ID parade,
to see if I could identify the man.

I was terrified not knowing whether I was about to see the
man in the bandana again or Foxxy's fake brother.

Daddy cancelled his meetings and said he would stay in the
waiting area of the police station, suspecting that he should stay
nearby in case I needed him.

After checking in at the front desk, I followed a police officer to the witness waiting room. Another woman, short, dark, and plump, was already there. Our eyes locked, and I didn't need words to know that she was here to ID the man, too. Was she one of the women Catherine knew, or another? If another victim, that made six of us now. Six women.

Despite there being chairs spread out around the room, she and I sat side by side. I had so many questions I wanted to ask, but I was unsure what was allowed.

I told her my name, that had to be safe enough, and she introduced herself, too.

"I heard the police set a trap for him," she then said, a hand cupped over her mouth, her eyes straying toward the door and back. I guessed she was uncertain, too, what information we were allowed to share.

"After the raid on his house?" I asked in a hushed voice.

"Yeah. He was on bail, bail for other assaults, I heard."

I gasped. "How many assaults?"

"Mi nuh kno. Are you gay?" she asked.

I nodded.

She said she was bisexual, and she'd only told her boyfriend that she'd been robbed. "I couldn't tell him bout di attack, yuh know."

"Do you know who we are ID'ing? The man in the bandana or Foxxy's brother?"

"The man in the bandana."

A shiver moved through me. This man had the gun.

She had supposedly overheard police saying that Foxxy's fake brother hadn't shown for his bail hearing but that he was wanted for assault, too. "He's still out there," she whispered.

"Yuh know wah di guy ina di bandana look like?" I asked. "Yuh did see 'im face or sup'm?"

"Not him full face, but I think enough to mek a ID."

The woman was called into the ID room first.

While she was gone, I sat, still, quiet, alone, staring at the ceiling, the yellow stains, and then my sneakers — black-and-white Converse knock-offs. I wrung my hands together, which felt stripped down and exposed without my silver ring.

Outside the room, in the hallway, the shuffling and usual commotion had gone quiet, as if everyone, not just me, were holding their breaths. When the woman came back, her eyes were red and tears had smeared her makeup. "I couldn't do it," she sobbed. "I couldn't ID him. Mi cud'n recognize 'im face."

On shaking legs, I stood up. It was now my turn.

When I entered the screening room, I jumped. There were six or seven men, all behind a window, standing up close, not far away like I'd seen on television crime dramas. I started to exit the room, momentarily convinced the glass that separated us wasn't one-sided, and that all these men, including the attacker, could see me as clearly as I could see them.

"Tek all di time yuh need," the police officer facilitating the ID parade said. As if sensing my fear, he added, "You can stand right up to the window and still they can't see you."

I timidly approached the window.

As I moved from man to man, I recalled those hands; rough, smelling of oil and marijuana, pushing me down, down, to the ground.

"Palms up an den palms down," I asked the police officer to tell the men.

I singled out four of the men for being too short, too tall, too skinny, or too fat. There were two I couldn't decide on.

I asked each of the men to turn to the side, so I could view their profiles. Afterward, I stepped up close to the window and walked slowly from one man to the next, studying their eyes. In my mind I saw them, all over again, the eyes, empty, soulless even. Someone who could commit so many crimes and still have a soul was beyond me.

I knelt down in front of each man, forcing myself to remember, *remember*, when I was forced, naked and raw, to kneel in front of the man.

"Can you have each man say, '*Pussyhole go ova de-so*,'" I finally asked the officer.

I asked one man to repeat it.

"And again," I demanded, my heart beating fast.

"That's him," I finally said, pointing. "That's him."

* * *

The station was breathing again. Like an ant colony, there was scurried movement.

As I made my way back to the waiting room, I caught one officer telling another: "She dweet. She point 'im out."

Back in the witness waiting room, I was alone, the woman having left. I was about to sit down, when I spied on a table a newspaper that hadn't been there before. I picked it up. It was open to an article from two years earlier about a man who was accused of attacking *more than a hundred* women and girls. As soon as I read the name, Ronique Raymond, I heard someone outside say the name, too.

He was my attacker. He had been out and sexually assaulting women and girls for years. He was the one who destroyed my friend Sasha and so many others of us, too.

Ronique Raymond was the man in the bandana with the beanie cap. He had been a suspect for sexual assaults for several years, the article said. Each time out on bail, with his victims unable or too afraid to ID him. Someone had clearly left the newspaper for me to find.

Ronique Raymond.

* * *

The St. Catherine police are warning parents that a popular website is being used by sexual predators to lure teenagers and young adults.

… 23-year-old Ronique Raymond, a labourer, of Kitson Town in the parish, who is now before the courts on 109 sexual offences, all relating to the internet.…

The police believe Mr. Raymond is the mastermind luring young women between the ages of 15 and 21 through the internet.

— Radio Jamaica News, November 2007

CHAPTER SIXTEEN

A book is from your heart and mind,
it is your love put to words.

— *Michael Anthony*

I met Ana. She had a slim, toned body and was not tall, five foot. But she didn't feel tiny, just shorter than me; if she stood directly in back of me, no one would be able to see her at all.

I was fourteen. She was sixteen.

I didn't notice her at first.

We were in the same English literature class.

It was September, I remember that. The teacher was talking about how we needed to be structured and attentive in the coming school year so that we would receive strong recommendations for our courses for the following year. The recommendations from each subject teacher were necessary to sit the Caribbean Secondary Education Certificate exam. The more courses and high grades a student had, the better their opportunities for university placements and jobs.

I was bored, wanting to get right into the curriculum. The covers of the books we were doing looked fascinating and I wanted to dive in: Shakespeare, *The Merchant of Venice* and *Macbeth*; John Steinbeck's *The Pearl*; and Michael Anthony's *Green Days by the River*, a coming-of-age book about a Trinidadian boy.

Sasha was not in this class. In fact, none of the students from the year before were.

Since I knew no one, I didn't gossip during breaks. My time was mine and I was able to read ahead. I was happy that our curriculum included literature from the Caribbean. I liked the books with characters that looked like us, talked like us, that shared our past and present experiences.

Ana, sitting in front of me, swivelled in her seat and waved her hand in front of my book to get my attention. I was initially surprised at her appearance and how I hadn't noticed her before. She was beautiful, with processed hair, a long slender dancer's neck and pudding-smooth skin. She introduced herself, her voice slightly husky, like she had a sore throat, yet feminine.

The seat beside me was empty; the student who had been sitting there gone for break. Ana grabbed my former desk-mate's books and knapsack, plopped them down on her desk and then quickly sat down, acting, when the others returned to their seats, like she'd been there the entire time.

"I have been watching you," she whispered as the teacher started lecturing again.

I wish I could have said I had been watching her, too. I wish

I had. Something about her reminded me of the calmness and beauty of dusk.

Ana coughed and, as she did so, skidded her chair until its wooden legs were flush against mine. Our own legs, bare beneath our tunics, rubbed up against each other. I kept my eyes looking forward, unblinking.

I couldn't focus on the lesson, not that it mattered. I had long mastered spelling, grammar, basic properties of an essay, elements of a news story.

I wanted Sasha. I started to reach for my phone to text her to ask if she knew Ana and, more importantly, what I should do. But Ana was so close, I could feel her breath on my cheek. She'd see anything I wrote.

Ana wrapped a foot around my ankle. My back stiffened. From the corner of my eye, I could see her scribbling in her notebook, the end of her pencil chewed. Her handwriting I thought was neat, a controlled, legible cursive. Mine was messy and fast, and most of the time illegible to anyone but me.

In the days that came after, spilling into time fast and uncontrolled, I noticed that Ana had puffy lips, which she'd coat in lip balm, reminding me of Annetta's lips. When the teacher announced that we would be moving on to our first book of the term, *Macbeth*, I could take no more.

Images of Amelia's assault of words came crashing down around me as I wrote as neat as I could in the corner of Ana's notebook: "Are you into me?" I was sure she was going to respond "no," and tell me to get lost.

She quietly giggled. I melted.

"Yes. Very much so," she wrote back. "Yes."

* * *

Ana and I would take our lunches nestled up beside each other in the music room or on a concrete garden bench behind one of the classrooms where no one could see us; our legs draped over each other's, our torsos touching. We shared our lunches — cheese Danish or beef patty and coco bread, fried chicken and fries. Sometimes, I'd only have candy and she'd scold me for not eating healthy, while we talked about music, Ana introducing me to pop, blues, jazz, and R & B. And I would help her with her homework and talk with her about my love of God.

She told me she had thought she couldn't have both: be a lesbian and be faithful to the church and Jesus. But then she had discovered online organizations, many located in the United States, including church denominations, that challenged the Christian view that homosexuality was a sin. There were even Bible verses these organizations suggested that contradicted the clobber passages, like Ruth 1:16–17 and the story of Jonathan and David's love in 1 and 2 Samuel.

My first proper kiss was with Ana. It was a few weeks before the break for Christmas holidays. No one was around. We were in the bathroom and were washing our hands when the quietness dawned on us. We moved closer to each other, her arm brushing against mine, the hair on both our skins standing up. Our lips touched briefly and I quickly jumped back out of fear that someone would walk into that bathroom at that very moment.

It came as a surprise and I felt awkward and embarrassed, sure that Ana would be turned off by my lack of skill or sour breath, but she wasn't. She kissed me again, her tongue finding its way into my mouth.

We became one.

Ana introduced me to the word *femme*, which was her; aware of and comfortable in her femininity, but saucy at the same time. I wanted to ask her how many girls she'd been with. But I was too afraid to ask her too much, to pry, in case she thought my questions boring and needy.

No fantasy could have prepared me for the intensity of my wanting her. I could barely hold myself together in our English Literature class, as we prepared to perform *Macbeth* in the auditorium. I was cast as one of the three witches: "When the hurly-burly's done, when the battle's lost and won."

I could smell and taste Ana when we were not together. I finally believed I had discovered that love Amoy had talked about: to me it was beauty. A beauty that warms and melts the cold inside away. To wake up and know someone else was interested in my life, in my body, in my mind and laughter, carried me on some cloud, where I felt nothing was impossible.

All my worries, gone.

All my fears, disappeared.

When we weren't in class together, we'd write each other notes, sometimes long letters, that we'd hand off to each other between classes.

At New Year's, we texted that we loved each other, and we wanted to get married one day.

Despite not thinking I had done much work at all that term, my marks soared. While it was hard to concentrate on homework as all I thought about was Ana, in those few moments in between, I did more than I would have had she not been in my life. I wrote a paper, perhaps the best of my life, on how Lady Macbeth was *not* a feminist icon. That she was a distorted version of masculine meanness, that her power was to be controlling and vindictive, because no matter what freedom she may have thought she had, her husband still held all the power in their marriage, lives, kingdom. I even wrote that maybe Lady Macbeth became so mean because her own identity was being suppressed, and perhaps she liked women?

I then ripped the paper up, fearing I had gone too far, too modern, too evolved.

Nonetheless, I had this feeling that, until Ana, I had just been preparing for life. I wasn't really living, I was waiting.

* * *

Around the end of January, Ana started sitting somewhere else in our class together and skipping our lunches. For the first week, I wondered if it had something to do with me. Had I said or done something to turn her off? So I'd call her. Leave a voice message, a text, even an email, although I knew she didn't look at her email frequently.

No reply. Soon, I felt I had become not even a ghost, but a nonentity — like I never existed at all, which made me question whether anything between us was real or not. Had I imagined everything? I went back to our texts to remind myself she actually had said she loved me.

One day I caught up to her walking to the bus stop after school.

"What's going on?" I asked.

"Busy," she replied. "Sorry. I'll reply to your messages tonight." She then breezed off, her bus was there, crowded and cramped, but she still hopped on, despite another bus, empty, right on its heels.

"Tonight" came and went. No call. No text.

I started to spin. My head, like my thoughts, would pound and circle, irrational, hysterical, needy, crazy.

She doesn't like me anymore.

There is a good explanation for this.

We are in love. She's scared.

I am ugly. I'm not good enough.

It's okay.

It's not okay.

Eventually I couldn't take any more. I needed answers.

At lunch one day, I decided to look for her in our Home Economics classroom.

The bench behind the classroom.

Then the music room.

When I arrived, the door was slightly ajar. I heard laughter, giggles, her unmistakable cooing — cooing like she would do in my ear, like a dove, gentle and light, a flutter of a dainty wing, and hushed words like "I love you."

Love.

But with another girl.

When I pushed open the door, I saw that Ana's legs and the other girl's were entwined. I didn't know who the other girl was. But they were kissing each other. Kissing deeply, intimately, like we used to do.

French kissing.

It was the day before Valentine's Day that Ana told me we were breaking up. She loved someone else.

CHAPTER SEVENTEEN

Love is the will to extend one's self for the purpose of
nurturing one's own or another's spiritual growth ... We do
not have to love. We choose to love.

— *M. Scott Peck*, The Road Less Traveled: A New Psychology
of Love, Traditional Values and Spiritual Growth

After that, I couldn't even look at Ana.

Betrayal buried itself deep inside me.

The anger.

The guilt, that I'd done something to make her not like me.
That I was at fault.

If I hadn't called so many times, I would have come across
as less clingy.

Maybe if I hadn't talked so much about scriptures?

No, Ana was at fault. She was a flirt, and unfaithful, and a liar.

The pounding, ricocheting thoughts were not like when I
had seizures. These thoughts hit me hard and in a place of total

awareness. It was like I had several voices inside my head, and none were rational.

The first time I sought release by cutting was toward Easter. I had punched the case of an R & B mash-up CD. The tough plastic had broken through the soft skin on my knuckles. Thin lines of broken flesh emerged and slivers of blood lay on top of the cuts.

I welcomed the light throbbing pain; it distracted me from thinking about Ana. The anger slowly seeped away. Only to return, so I cut myself again for relief.

My grades plummeted. I wasn't paying attention in any of my classes.

My essays were returned with Cs and Ds.

My history teacher pulled me aside, asking if everything was okay at home.

Miss Brown, curvy Miss Brown, called me in for a meeting, wanting to talk confidentially about my declining school performance.

I stopped paying attention in class, and extracurricular activities no longer interested me.

But I couldn't tell Miss Brown. I felt too ashamed to confide in her, not that I was a lesbian, but that I had lost Ana — that my first love had loved me and then dismissed me, like I was nothing more than an old Styrofoam cup.

I thought of killing myself, on the days I got home and no one was there, when I'd seen Ana with her new love; the flick of the hair, the way they looked at each other, their eyes full of longing and lust, the hand holding.

I prayed to God, asking, "Why? Why bring beauty into my life to just take it away?

"Why leave me with such a hole, like the chi chi do the old rotting wood of our colonial homes and buildings?"

Chi chi, Sasha told me, was the name also hurled at lesbians and gays on the island. *Chi chi.* I was nothing more than a termite — Ana had proved that to be so.

* * *

I barely passed that year, doing well enough that I didn't have to repeat courses but not well enough, if I kept it up, to get me into a good college or university when I graduated the following year. Mommy and Daddy discussed my changing schools, believing that part of the problem was the hour-and-a-half commute each way. At least if I cut out the long bus rides, I'd have more time for homework. Mommy and Daddy said they were also going to hire me a tutor in Spanish and Literature, a woman named Miss Campbell, who tutored and taught school part-time. I dared not tell them that my grades sucked because I'd given up. What was the point of living if there was no love?

Ocho Rios High School was located twenty-three minutes from our house. The school was co-ed, and I was familiar with the layout of the classrooms as the North Eastern Missionary Conference of Christian Brethren churches had used the facility for our week-long sleepover camps. It was a sprawling campus, with four two-storey blocks of classrooms. Some of the classrooms had olden style wooden benches seating two students at a desk. Other classrooms had the more updated single-chair-and-desk format of my previous schools. Palm trees, Jamaican almond, ixora shrubs, and other trees, bushes, and flowers made Ocho Rios High School look like it was in the middle of a flowered fairy-tale garden.

I entered Fifth Form (Grade 11), mad, cutting, viewing everyone I met initially as an enemy. I had no Sasha. I had no Ana, who had moved to Florida to live with an aunt. Or at least that was what Sasha told me. Even though I was hurt and confused by Ana, the thought of her being near was still comforting. Now she was hundreds of miles away and kissing another girl.

Some of the Ocho Rios girls started laying into me right away, saying that, since I had come from the all-girls St. Hilda's, I must be gay. Natasha, a plump girl with processed hair that she would catch up in a bun and paste the baby hairs down with hair jam, and who when not in school uniform wore tight pants and belly skin blouses, seemed to have it in the worst for me. She'd try to trip me as I walked along the corridor to my class-rooms, her group of girls standing by giggling, ready to burst out laughing if I fell. In class she would throw balls of paper at the back of my head. My tutoring sessions with Miss Campbell were unproductive. She tried both academically to inspire me and, as if sensing my deeper problems, attempted to get me to open up. She would talk about herself and the world, and I got the sense she was an activist of sorts. But I wasn't interested in her deep conversations.

Natasha had a boyfriend: a star two-hundred-metre runner and one of the runners on the school's relay team. He was tall, had rippling muscles he'd show off when training, and a wide, toothy smile like an actor. As a stealthy eavesdropper, I heard enough whispers to get that Natasha and her boyfriend were sexually active.

I wanted revenge on Ana.

I wanted the girls at Ocho Rios High to leave me alone.

I wanted to move around the school, unnoticed, like a duppy. A duppy who had been crossed. Natasha's boyfriend, Trevor, had been hitting on me from the second week of school. It was easy to play along, inviting his attention, especially in front of Natasha. I encouraged his flirting, which fuelled him to escalate his advances, brushing up beside me in class or, when passing behind me, pressing himself against my butt. He kissed me once, his masculine jawline, smells, tongue so unlike the softness and warmth of Ana. One day, after school had been out for hours, we hid behind the building and he went down on me.

My ruse worked. Natasha found out and broke up with her boyfriend after that.

Natasha left me alone: the taunting stopped completely. If I was walking down the hall and she the other way, she'd turn on her heels, dart into a classroom or the toilets. I had now become a Genna (high-ranking boss), or maybe people had just figured out to leave me alone.

Her friends, her girls, wanted to get to know me. I made small talk and then left them. I wasn't interested in friends.

Trevor wanted more, more with me. But my point was proven and I didn't want to go further with him. I started avoiding him, making excuses that I had homework and extracurricular activities.

I eventually got my wish: privacy, to merge with the school, to walk both unseen and feared and envied. And that is how I spent the start of the school year at Ocho Rios High, in part wishing I could actually become a duppy, doing enough school work and participating in church activities to not draw attention, but not really living at all.

* * *

Ana was back from Florida.

And messaging me. :-) :-) :-) :-s

Apologizing. :-(:-[:'(:-/

Wanting to see me, touch me, kiss me all over again. ;-) ;-) :-* :-* <3 <3 <3

She was home, to finish high school and her final year of exams. She missed me. She had made a mistake. She said she'd been foolish, young, and seduced by the other girl. I was her true love.

A fool? I went back, like even just the "hi" in her text message was enough for me to rush into her arms, inhaling now the palm and orange blossoms of Florida, where she had just left. Her body was more compact, toned, from Pilates and the exercises Americans do, she told me. Her hair was still processed but long, stretching down her back.

She said that when she was in the United States she'd attended a gay wedding.

She introduced me to more websites on LGBTQ and Christianity. She told me there were gay male and female ministers in the Metropolitan Community Churches.

"You can become a minister if you want," she beamed. Ana knew my deep faith and had always urged me to be a leader in the church. But I'd never entertained thoughts that it was possible, not just because I was female and my church had no female pastors, but also because I was gay. I thought of a passage in Jeremiah, 1:5: "Before I formed thee in the belly I knew thee; and before thou camest forth out of the womb I sanctified thee, and I ordained thee a prophet unto the nations."

"We can do it," she said. "I want to go to Canada though. Toronto. They have clubs and restaurants where we can go and be open."

"I can work in computer support since I will study information technology after school," I said enthusiastically.

"I'll work as a waitress while you get your IT degree to support us; then you can get a better job like in programming or something, while I go to school. I want to study nursing at the University of Toronto."

We were sixteen and eighteen, planning our lives together away from Jamaica and the chi chi label, the buggery laws, and the anti-gay Biblical rhetoric.

Shortly after Valentine's Day, a year after our breakup, Ana and I had sex. It was at my house, in my room, on my bed. No one was home. We started with kissing that seemed more intense, more hungry, than the first time we kissed. Our clothes landed in a pile on the floor by our feet, only our panties remained. I kissed her neck as she held the back of my head. Kissing along her body, my hand on her hip, I could feel her nipples harden as I pressed myself against her. She thrusted her hips toward me and I could feel the heat between her thighs. I brought myself back to her lips and enjoyed the feel of her soft flush lips against mine, her tongue engaging mine. I fumbled blindly to reach between her thighs and feel her wetness, her other lips, slippery to the touch ...

She sent me texts after that, about how great it was — how she could still taste me on her lips and feel me around her even when we were not together.

Being back with Ana was being seen, held, and heard again. It takes a lot to trust a God I cannot see, a Holy Spirit, whispering to me in such a hushed voice that I question whether I've heard correctly. But Ana, she was living proof that God had answered my prayers, bringing love I could give to another person.

I surrendered totally to her, to us.

I now got that my family, including sisters, had no clue how to search our browser histories. I spent long nights at the computer in our home library downstairs researching LGBT-affirming theology and Bible and ministerial courses I could take, without fearing my family seeing and confronting me when I was not ready to answer their questions. I wanted to become a better lover, too, so I was also searching for how to have sex as a lesbian. That's how I got introduced to pornography.

* * *

I texted Ana that my parents and sisters were out for the night at a church event that I knew would run late. She came over and we had sex for a second time. When we were finished and Ana had pulled back on her bra, inner shirt, and skirt, we made our way downstairs to find something to eat. As soon as I closed the fridge, I heard it: the closing of the front door.

The jingling of the keys. The clip of my mom's shoe heels against the ceramic tiles.

I went into a frantic checklist. Ana's backpack was in my room. Good.

How did we leave the bed? Completely dishevelled, the top sheet on the floor, the fitted sheet dishevelled and draping off the side. My pillows? Somewhere on the floor? Our clothes, still in a heap on the floor. *Shit!*

Mommy called out to me and started making her way to the kitchen. *Fuck!*

I pushed Ana into the laundry room. Not often, but occasionally, Mommy returned early because she was tired and wanted a few hours to herself. As she came toward the kitchen, Mommy called out that she was early so she could start the laundry.

You've got to be kidding me!

I stood at the wall between the dining room and laundry room. "You can't go around there," I said.

"Why not?" she asked, trying to push past me.

"Please just don't go around there."

"Who's in the house, Angeline?" she asked, her voice raised, like she was calling out to whoever I was hiding. "Why I can't go in the laundry room? Who you got in the house?"

As I barred her way — for now I was heavier than Mommy — she paced the kitchen. At one point, when she turned, she was holding a machete.

"Angeline!" she shouted. "Who you have in here?"

"Mommy, please. Please, Mommy," I begged, getting down on my knees and holding my hands out in front of me like in prayer. "I can't let you go there. Please go upstairs. I will tell you, I promise."

I thought I was going to pee on myself.

Mommy put the machete down and walked to the dining room door, fuming, and then stopped because she saw them. Ana's shoes. "Angeline," she said, spinning back toward me.

"Please, Mommy, please go upstairs, I will tell you, but later."

Mommy studied me, long and hard, her eyes probing and darting. I could tell she was at a loss as to what to do. Trust me?

Or bulldoze past me and assume things for herself, breaking whatever bond we had between us? After what felt like hours but was probably seconds, she finally relented. With a sigh and a shake of her head, she went upstairs.

When Ana left the house, I found Mommy in her bedroom. I sat on the bed. My mother asked if I had had a boy in the house. She asked next who was in the house and what was going on. I said I had a friend over, and we were doing school work.

"Then why all the secrecy?" she asked.

"Because I hadn't asked permission."

I knew I was lying, but I couldn't tell her I had my girlfriend over.

Mommy, to my relief, didn't ask any further questions. I didn't think I had convinced her or gained her trust. Maybe she stopped because she didn't want to stir up more trouble with me. After all, she had two other children and work and the church.

Either way, after that night, Ana and I found new places to meet up — friends' houses when their parents weren't home, even motel rooms, cheap rooms, since neither of us had much money. I didn't want to even think who'd been in there before us.

During my last semester of high school, I started volunteering with Jamaica AIDS Support for Life. I found telling Mommy and Daddy I was working or studying with friends was enough for them to trust me and let me live my life.

Ana and I texted a lot.

Every day.

Every half-hour of every day.

I lived and breathed for her.

Ana: I love kissing your neck
Angeline: I can't get enough of exploring your mouth
with my tongue
Ana: Ooooh I can feel you now
Angeline: I want to touch and kiss every part of you. I
want to feel your legs around my hips
Ana: I fall asleep touching myself thinking about the
last time ...
Angeline: I can't wait to see you tomorrow baby
Ana: ...
Angeline: Ana ...? You gone sleep?
Ana: My mom read our messages
Angeline: What? How? Are you ok?
Ana: I'm ok, she beat me up real bad

The following morning, as I was about to leave home for school, front door open, shuffling papers into my backpack, my phone rang. It was Mommy, who was already at work.

"Angeline, DO NOT GO. I heard that somebody's mother is looking for you to beat you up."

CHAPTER EIGHTEEN

August 2009

After I ID'd Ronique, the police could not tell me whether he was in prison or out on bail. He'd been out on bail, free, when he did this to me and Sasha. I had not been called to do any further lineups, either, which meant that Foxxy's fake brother and Foxxy were still at large, too. *How many more victims until they're brought to justice?* So for weeks after ID'ing the assailant, I'd wake perspiring in the night, panting, thinking for a moment I was having a seizure, my body shaking, having been jolted awake by the image of his face, Ronique Raymond's, puncturing any dreams I might have been having. My eyes would dart around the darkened room, sure he was standing in a corner, or outside the window, that gun with the green-taped handle in his hand. I'd even check the earth around the house and by the mango tree the next morning to see if there were footprints, evidence of him having been there.

I didn't leave the house. I began staying up well past my parents to double- and sometimes triple-check that the doors and windows were locked. But my vivid imagination still found ways for him, *him*, to enter my house.

I had by now finished high school and was taking courses in computer science. But I started researching online options for studying law, having decided I wanted to represent clients like myself: in need of being believed, in need of a justice system that supported rather than condemned them, in need of someone fighting in their corner.

I reflected on the passages of the Bible that I had come to hold close to me. These passages became like a coat, keeping me warm and the shadows of storms away, confirming for me that Jesus and God accepted all of us, and I was being guided and supported.

In Romans, for instance, "For I am persuaded, that neither death, nor life, nor angels, nor principalities, nor powers, nor things present, nor things to come, nor height, nor depth, nor any other creature, shall be able to separate us from the love of God, which is in Christ Jesus our Lord."

Mommy and Daddy tried to keep family life as normal as possible as we waited to find out whether Ronique Raymond was going to go to trial or not. My hope was that he would plead guilty and spend a very long time in prison. I didn't want to see him in court.

Foxxy never contacted me again to meet up. I wasn't sure if this was a positive sign or negative, like she knew, he knew, and they were going to come after me.

As Latoya, Toni, and I had grown, our nightly devotional before bed had become less and less frequent. We would pray before meals, always, having God bless the food, thanking Him for giving us life, meaning, sustenance. Now, in the aftermath of the assault — in that tired period where night seems heaviest — there was a quiet creeping up on me that scared me. Mommy and Daddy, perhaps sensing, perhaps knowing, had devotion every night. Mommy would walk in as we were finishing a television show — I hardly paid attention to what was on TV, as I was constantly anticipating what would happen when my case went to court. She'd place her Bible and her Our Daily Bread Devotional on the armrest of the sofa. And then we'd start. Sometimes Daddy would ask all three of us girls to pray, other times, just one of us. Mommy would give him a short passage to read from the devotional, like 1 Peter 5:6–11, ensuring that nothing was longer than a paragraph or two because Daddy would go on and on lecturing all night if he could. Then Daddy would conclude with his own prayer, like he was gift-wrapping and putting a bow on top of a present we were lifting up to God.

These were the only times I felt safe, where my mind wasn't moving a thousand miles a minute, descending downward, *downward.*

This silence was nothing like I had experienced before. My mind was full of duppies that walked beside me and I could not shake them, blind, deaf, hurting, stealing … taking. I'd jump at the sound of a car horn outside, a weed whacker, or the front door opening; Daddy returning from work, my sisters from school.

Prayer, only prayer, settled me, gave me some reprieve from the internal noise, allowed me to continue my online researching and application to study law through the University of London distance program.

And then the call came. Officer Cox said a date had been set for the trial. Mommy had to accompany me and testify as well, since she was the first person I had spoken to about the assault.

"So there is a trial?" I asked, my voice weak, pensive, needing to know if he was at least in prison until the trial.

"Yes," said Officer Cox. "The man you ID'd is pleading innocent."

*　*　*

Mommy and I had to leave early, before Latoya and Toni were up, Daddy stretching his legs, groggy eyed, yawning as he hugged us goodbye on the driveway. Dawn was just breaking through the haze left over from the night.

The trial was to be held in Kingston, in one of the courthouses downtown.

Mommy and I said very little as she drove, at first a lone car on the road, until near Kingston the streets became awash with trucks and motorbikes, ancient Volkswagen bugs beside current Toyotas, sitting in traffic alongside cyclists pushing their way through the fumes to get to work.

I could taste the pollution. In St. Ann's Bay, the breeze was always blowing away the stenches of modern living. In Kingston, it was like oil and garbage fumes hung in the air.

We circled the courthouse a few times looking for parking. And that's when my fear really set in: I was sure a sniper was sitting atop a nearby building, waiting for me.

Once parked, Mommy and I made our way slowly to the building, and my entire body tightened, waiting for the bullet that was not shot on the day of the assault to come to me now.

Through security, Mommy and I moved to the second floor and the courtroom assigned to my case. The courthouse was a flurry of activity: mostly men, in their long court robes and the grey or white wigs that had to be worn by lawyers and judges deliberating cases. For a brief moment, I thought back to Kimmy, of my girls, and her aspiration to become a lawyer herself. The courthouse was abuzz with men, carrying oversized briefcases and tugging behind them carry-on suitcases full of court documents, zigzagging into and out of halls, stopping to talk, to make a plea bargain with another lawyer. As far as I could see there were no female lawyers, and we needed to be represented.

Officer Smith met Mommy and me outside the courtroom. She informed us that we had to wait to enter until we were called to testify. The three of us sat on a wooden bench, across from the courtroom's front door.

My pulse quickened every time the door opened, my eyes stretching to get a look at the man, *that man.*

Mommy went into the courtroom first.

Officer Smith and I, in quiet voices, talked about the case and my testimony. I went over that day, starting with arriving at the snack shop and Foxxy's fake brother coming to get me instead of Foxxy.

"When I saw the gun, I froze," I told Officer Smith.

"Don't say 'froze.'"

"Why?" I asked Officer Smith.

"Because the defence could say you don't remember, you were too dazed, too 'frozen' in fear to recall the crime."

"Okay," I replied, my mind stretching to the *Law and Order* episodes where witnesses were deposed by the prosecution before testifying. I guessed this was my deposition, this conversation with Officer Smith.

Officer Smith and I finished our conversation and I started pacing the hallway, back and forth, wringing my hands, just wanting to leave or get it over with. Anything but wait. It felt like Mommy was in the courtroom for hours.

When Mommy finally emerged, her eyes looked heavy, her body sluggish. I closed my eyes: Luciano's "Lord Give Me Strength" came to mind.

The courtroom was small, with several rows of empty chairs and then the prosecution and defence desks.

There was no jury, no spectators, just a few police officers I didn't recognize, and a judge and the lawyers wearing their robes and wigs. A court officer escorted me to the witness stand. I kept my eyes downcast the entire time, fearing that if I looked up, I'd see him, *him*, and run away.

I gave my oath to tell the truth, with a hand on the Bible. I then sat down, my legs underneath me, trembling.

"Can you identify the man who attacked you?" the prosecution asked. I looked up, at Ronique Raymond, who was staring, glaring at me, his head slightly tilted, his eyes piercing. I fought the urge to look away, to say I didn't recognize the man, when I clearly did.

I was afraid.

The prosecution laid out my possessions, still in their clear plastic evidence bags.

All the while I was having flashbacks of the day, *that day*.

"Pray for me," he had said, pushing my head, pushing me, to do things to him. "You're a Christian, pray for me."

For a moment, I closed my eyes, willing my mind to stop

showing me, reminding me in such graphic detail. "Please, God, let me just give the facts …"

The defence attorney's turn came.

"Did you wear this ring," he said, holding up the plastic evidence bag with my ring in it, "on your thumb, the way lesbians do?"

I bit my lip. How should I answer? Sometimes? Then I recalled that Officer Smith had said to only give yes and no answers.

"No," I eventually replied, which was true. I often wore the ring on my index finger, occasionally moving it to my thumb only when I was around people I knew identified with my orientation.

I could sense Ronique Raymond, in his suit, slightly too big, likely borrowed, instead of the grease-stained clothes he wore on that day, staring me down hard, trying to make me falter, threatening me with his eyes.

Next question: "How can you be sure this man is the man who attacked you?"

I took a deep breath, Officer Smith having warned me I would likely have to explain how I identified the man. I answered that I recognized his eyes, his height, his hands, and his voice.

"Why were you in Spanish Town? You are from St. Ann's Bay … why so far away from home?"

"I was meeting a friend."

The entire time, I avoided his gaze. But the entire time, I sensed Ronique Raymond's stare never left me.

After, *after,* a police officer led me from the courtroom, to Mommy, we went for some food. We didn't speak, neither of us, for the longest time, and when we finally did it was to pray.

* * *

A few weeks later I got the phone call. It was Officer Cox. Daddy was not home. Mommy was making dinner. Officer Cox asked me to sit down, to take a minute. I looked around — my sisters were doing homework in their rooms.

"Tell me," I asked. "Just tell me."

He had been found guilty.

Ronique Raymond was guilty.

CHAPTER NINETEEN

We are going to emancipate ourselves from mental slavery,
because whilst others might free the body, none but ourselves
can free the mind. Mind is your only ruler, sovereign. The man
who is not able to develop and use his mind is bound to be the
slave of the other man who uses his mind.

— *Marcus Garvey*

Mommy texted me to meet her at the Ocho Rios Jerk Center.

I thought she was hungry.

When I arrived, the restaurant was not crowded. I didn't
see Mommy in the main section, so I moved toward the right
side of the building where there were gazebos, wooden benches, and tables.

I then stopped in my tracks. Sitting at a table, heads lowered,
were Mommy, Daddy, Ana, a woman I suspected was Ana's mom,
although I had never met her, and the stepdad she had talked to
me about. They were sitting at one of the gazebos. Mommy and

Daddy on one of the wooden benches. Ana's mom and stepdad on another. Ana was sitting alone, leaving one bench open for me.

How did Mommy and Daddy come to be here? How did Ana's mom get our phone number to communicate? Why was I not told? Even if Ana's mom hadn't found me to beat me up, this was a betrayal.

As I neared, my eyes moved from her family to Ana, whose arms and hands were bruised. The skin on both of her wrists was raw, like she'd been dragged or held tight and shaken.

She would not meet my gaze, no matter how much I willed her to do so.

Before I even sat down, Ana's mom was on me. "Angeline, look at her, big girl, twice the size of little Ana, she corrupted her. I know. Ana likes boys, this is Angeline's fault." As she spoke, she looked at me, well, not at my eyes, but at my body, deciding that because I was butch, and bigger, obviously this was my doing, that I had lured their feminine, dainty daughter into a relationship.

Daddy spoke next, clearing his throat and, I could tell, trying to remain calm. Ana, he said, was two years older than me. I was vulnerable, a child, compared to her, who must have been the one to tempt me into something I did not want.

I fought the urge to roll my eyes.

Ana still would not look at me.

I glanced around the restaurant as Ana's mom and my parents bantered back and forth on who was to blame, while her stepdad kept his head down. It was clear that the table had been chosen to offer some privacy. Maybe whoever had arranged this meetup expected the conversation to go badly. Maybe he or she expected shouting and screaming. Maybe it was Daddy and he thought he'd have to stop Ana's mom from becoming physically violent. Or maybe the simplest answer was the most honest one: they were probably all too embarrassed that they even needed to have this conversation.

Mommy and Daddy, obviously having been prepared for this meeting, slipped a piece of paper across the table to Ana's mom. On it was the name of a therapist in St. Ann's Bay that worked with people who wanted to get rid of their "unwanted sexual attractions."

This was all boring to me. I just wanted to tell my parents and Ana's mom that Ana and I loved each other, and nothing was wrong with us. We were fine. We weren't going to hell. We weren't sinful. And we wanted to get married.

Ana was lifeless. Like she was bored, too. Or scared. I found myself thinking back to something my tutor, Miss Campbell, had said to me about how we initially respond to life-threatening events: fight, flight, or freeze. Ana was frozen.

Ana's mom wore blue jeans, a flowy blouse, and gold earrings. She was explaining to Daddy that she and her husband were God-fearing Christians, and that they had raised Ana well.

Daddy talked about our faith and how devoted I was to the church.

This argument went back and forth with Mommy raising and lowering her eyes, mouth open as if about to speak and then shutting it quickly. When she finally spoke, she raised a hand and said, "Enough … enough," pointing her finger at each of them. "What are we all going to do about this, to support our daughters to, well, become healthy again?"

I felt like sticking my tongue out of my mouth to imitate vomiting and yelling at them, "How are you going to support us as *lesbians*? What are we doing that straight boys and girls are not doing? Exploring relationships, their bodies, their loves and turn-ons, their discomforts?" Miss Campbell had said to me, "Angeline, you choose people, loves, relationships, to evolve, to lay your hurts and fears aside, to push you to be better."

"Why does a same-sex relationship," I wanted to yell, "not do this?"

I said nothing. But my eyes said a lot, as I went from person to person, gauging what their real agendas were.

With Ana's mom, I got the sense that she was trying to compensate for her irregular presence. She was one of the many parents who went abroad to create a better life for their child, but missed the day-to-day growth and development.

With Mommy and Daddy it was more complicated. I got the feeling they actually believed what they had been told in their churches about gays: that we were going to hell.

I guessed they, too, had read the yellow book. I hadn't ever thought about that. To them, I was probably stuck in that infantile state.

We finally left, the restaurant filling up with dinner patrons wanting jerk pork and chicken, rice and peas, and red peas soup. We, having ordered nothing, had not paid a cent for the use of their space. Ana's mom agreed that something needed to be done and thanked my parents for being so supportive. She left the restaurant, followed by Ana's stepdad, who looked confused, tired, and worn, and then Ana, tailing them like a duckling, skittish and scared.

As for me? On the car ride home, Mommy and Daddy told me they had spoken to the elders, discreetly, in private, to protect my reputation, and they had booked an appointment with a therapist at Family Life Ministries, a Christian therapy organization that, it wasn't said but I gathered from the description, was set up to convert gay youth. Conversion therapy. I was going to conversion therapy in Kingston.

A Few Weeks Later ...

The waiting room was painted blue, with sunlight streaming in through a large window. There was a small TV in the corner, on but at a low volume, playing one of the religious channels on cable. It could have been TBN. On a table in the middle of the room sat materials on becoming straight, books about the journey out of homosexuality, and pamphlets advertising upcoming workshop presentations on freeing the soul of sexual demons.

My counsellor introduced herself and explained her position as both a Christian and a therapist, saying her goal was to help young people get back on the right path that God had designed for them.

For Mommy and Daddy's sake, I had vowed I would try, *try*, to take this therapy seriously. But I had already read too much. I knew too much. I had read stories of people who tried to change and couldn't and of people who went to Exodus International, an American conversion therapy organization, and didn't have any success.

I was still wholly and completely in love with Ana. I wanted to have a life with Ana. Even before and after my therapy sessions, she and I would text back and forth, me giving her updates on the nonsense the therapist was going on about. We'd end by agreeing to meet up when we could steal ourselves away from the watchful gaze of our parents.

Most of the questions the therapist asked were directed toward my parents. She wanted to understand my childhood, how I was raised, what had led to my being gay.

"So your mother wasn't in the home a lot?" she asked me one day. Mommy was in the room and squirmed in her seat. Daddy's nostrils started to flare.

"I supported my wife going back to school. I support women being their fullest. My wife is my equal not my subordinate," he explained, when the therapist, taking notes the entire time, questioned Mommy's departure to get her degrees.

"So Angeline felt that she was mostly being raised by her father and Uncle Anthony?" the therapist pressed on.

"Um," Daddy said, narrowing his eyes and scratching his chin.

"So Angeline had no feminine role model in the house?"

Mommy's eyes were ringed in dark circles. She was chewing the side of her mouth, which I knew meant she was thinking real hard about what was being said; she would be blaming herself.

I wanted to end this calamity right then and there.

The therapist had thin lips, real thin. Her face was slim, too. She wore a baby-blue suit to each and every appointment, like this was a uniform, with open-toed sandals that revealed her chipped, unmanicured nails and bony feet.

It would have helped me if she had had any warmth to her. Instead, she was like a piece of beef Mommy would ask me to retrieve from the freezer for a stew. She wasn't just chilly, she was rock hard. I could find nothing endearing about this counsellor, including her voice, which was official, like she was conducting a cross-examination in court, like her job was to prove to us, all of us, that I was unwell, and that the problem was how I was raised.

"So Angeline lacked a maternal presence in the home for many years," she said at another meeting, the question sounding more like a statement. Every session always came back to this.

My therapist quoted Romans 6:23: "The wages of sin is death, but the gift of God is eternal life." My gayness was the result of sin, she would then say, the by-product of being human, but if I repented and changed my ways, God's gift of eternal life was still available to me. If I remained gay, I wouldn't have eternal life. "Don't you want to go to Heaven and be with your parents and sisters after you die?"

Another time she talked about the lonely life homosexuals led, saying they didn't have stable, long-lasting relationships. They didn't form families. They just had empty sexual experiences that had no meaning. Many of them were depressed and committed suicide. "Don't you want to have a family? Don't you want to have a stable, long-lasting relationship? Don't you want to be happy?"

Through all of this, I kept up on my reading, finding other sources, other websites, to debunk conversion therapy — some even calling it a human rights violation. I printed out and kept in a binder studies and documents that supported the biology of our sexual attractions.

Through my reading, I came to buy into the theory that our natural state of being, that of the first humans on the planet, involved living collectively, where everything was shared, and spirituality — not religion — was about understanding the

universe and our oneness with each other. Rituals and trad-
itions, often passed on to young people during rite-of-passage
ceremonies, emphasized the importance of respect and tolerance, connecting with nature and each other. In the dawn
of civilizations, through the chaos of just existing in a world
that could move from storms to deep freezes to intense heat,
facing the violence of nature and animals, people by necessity
had to come together. Early spirituality saw a higher power as
a blend of female and male energies, too, which I thought was
very cool.

The introduction of property changed all that. What was
once communal started to become owned by the people with the
brawn and courage to take it from others. And who were these
people? Men, by virtue of their physicality, and part of their
property eventually involved women — wives and children —
who were weaker physically. This can be seen most glaringly in
nineteenth-century North America, when rape was considered
sex by force by someone other than the woman's husband. It was
the husband who was seen as being wronged when his wife was
raped; his wife was not seen as the victim of the crime. Enslaved
African American women had no rights over what happened
to their bodies and thus could be assaulted at will because they
were owned by their masters. Even white women found it difficult to prove sexual assault without physical injuries, largely
because of all-male, all-white juries. Throughout modern history, women could not withhold sex from their husbands (this
continues even today in some parts of the world). The husband
owned his wife and her property as well as his daughter until
she was married. There was very little talk throughout history
of the rape of boys and men.

Property also shifted spirituality to religions that excluded, condemned, and judged instead of unifying and making whole. People were separated from nature. God was seen as fire and brimstone, and identity became based on clans, groups, and socio-economic status, which led to fear of others and ultimately war. To be a man became about how much one owned; how much wealth he could amass in such a hostile world. To be a female was to be submissive, to become a possession, to follow the rules of the dominant male groups.

A few months into my therapy, I brought my binder with all my documents. I went through the pages, summarizing each point and argument.

The therapist listened, or maybe pretended to listen. When I was done, she waved the papers away as nonsense, as arguments espoused by white liberals in America who were deliberately distorting God's words. She then referenced Romans 1, saying that just like the sinners in the Bible who knew the truth of God and ignored it, exchanging it for a lie, these people were doing the same. "These documents, these websites were written by homosexuals who want to justify their behaviours and continue to live in sin," she said. "It was not what God wanted for them."

She then gave me my first "conversion therapy" assignment. I had to go on a date with a boy.

I felt like laughing, but then I recalled Mommy and Daddy's looks during our other sessions, their sinking bodies, their sagging faces: this is what defeat looked like. It wasn't just that they were spending probably the equivalent of hundreds of American dollars for these sessions and the commute to Kingston every Saturday, but also that they believed the therapist's opinion that they had caused my homosexuality.

I knew exactly the right boy to see, too, to entertain slightly, so maybe I could do this ... for my parents. He was one of my friends who lived in Brown's Town, named Jerome. Whenever we saw each other, he would say he wanted a chance to get to know me better, because he liked me and my shape. Plus, he went to the Baptist church, so I felt I would be relatively safe with him, a good Christian boy, and not be forced to do anything.

* * *

For some reason I cannot explain, during my therapy sessions my mind would often wander to Miss Campbell and things she had said to me during our tutoring lessons that I ignored at the time. I was realizing that she seemed to understand me in a way others didn't, so I sent a text asking if we could talk, saying that I was going through some things and would appreciate her guidance. I needed an adult's perspective.

She replied quickly, saying she had heard what I was going through.

We scheduled a meeting for a Friday evening, after I finished volunteering at Jamaica AIDS Support for Life. Anal sex was against the law in Jamaica, with prison sentences of up to ten years, and most families in Jamaica, not just mine, raised children in a strict Christian faith that believed homosexuality was Biblically wrong. Many gay youth led hidden lives and, if discovered, were likely not allowed to remain in their homes. St. Ann's Bay didn't have a significant homeless problem the way the bigger cities did, but I came to learn through my volunteer work about couch surfing, and how a lot of gay youth move from house to house, not just of friends or good Samaritans, but with so-called sugar daddies. These tended to be older men, and they were often rough and even abusive at times. I had gone through a lengthy training program on how to talk to these youth, educate them on sexually transmitted diseases or infections (STDs or STIs), and build trust as a peer support for them, so they would feel comfortable telling me their stories and I could direct them to help when needed.

But while I loved my work, I needed a guide, too, as the conversion therapy was really messing with my brain. And I felt I couldn't help other youth if I couldn't process what I, too, was going through.

Miss Campbell and I walked for a bit, from the clock tower in the main section of Ocho Rios toward the beach. I was sipping a Pepsi; she, a bottle of water. Eventually we sat on a stone wall, our faces turned to the sea, watching the soft whitecaps, the gentle lapping of the waves as they cleansed the sand. Miss Campbell had been my tutor for about a year. For some reason, intuition I guess, I felt I could trust her, that even if she didn't agree with my lifestyle and choices, she didn't judge, either. I let it all out about the conversion therapy and how I was now dating Jerome, the Baptist boy with slobbering lips whose body odour, while not bad, made me feel sick to my stomach when he leaned in to kiss me. He and I had gone to a movie at the one movie theatre in Ocho Rios, and as soon as the lights dimmed, he had started groping me.

"Ah hated the feel of him on me," I said.

"I know. I hate it, too."

I swivelled my torso so I was now looking at her. In the setting orange sun, her eyes looked amber. Her hair was locked, which always fascinated me. Many Jamaicans, especially professionals, would never wear locs, because of the negative connotations around the hairstyle. In Jamaica, locs are associated with the Rastafarians, a religious movement started in the 1930s. In 1963, one year after Jamaica gained its independence from Great Britain, some Rastafarians were killed in what came to be called the Coral Gardens massacre. Miss Campbell, who called herself a social justice campaigner for ending violence against women and girls, had told me she wore locs as a sign of protest against government corruption and in solidarity with those demanding their right to live their lives the way they wanted.

"Are you gay, Miss Campbell?" I asked.

"Yes, I am," she said.

Like a light switch, my anger, hurt, feelings of betrayal toward Ana poured out like water, like it had merely been plugged up when she had returned to Jamaica from Florida. But now, in this second deceit, in which her mom had gotten into her phone and I was forced to do this ridiculous conversion therapy ...

"I want to remember the good of me and Ana; what she showed me about being lesbian and faith in America. Our touch. Our times together ... but it's getting harder and harder because I just remember all the pain." I was speaking so fast, so furiously, that I had to stop and catch my breath.

"You know you're such an amazing young lady," Miss Campbell said. Her voice was low and raspy, very sexy, which I hadn't noticed before or hadn't wanted to. She was still my tutor. "I don't see how Ana could have broken up with you the first time. I would never hurt you." She then moved, swiftly, into me, kissing me, light but long, sensual and strong. Now here was a woman who knew how to please.

I told Mommy and Daddy, after three months of Saturdays spent in Kingston having the lady with feet like the skeleton of a mackerel preaching at me, that I was quitting counselling. They were wasting their money and I just couldn't take the pain it was causing them, as every session was driven back somehow to them and their bad parenting.

I texted Jerome and thanked him for our dates but said that I didn't want to see him anymore.

I broke up with Ana. I couldn't in my heart trust her, not again, not anymore. I probably hadn't even really trusted her the second time, I'd just been desperate and vulnerable.

I started to date Miss Campbell.

CHAPTER TWENTY

I stand
In a fold of time
And I slip knowing,
the unknown will catch me
in my becoming.

— *Miss Campbell*

Summer came hot, humid, and steamy. I was seventeen and landed my first paying job, at Dunn's River Falls. My official title was customer support liaison; I was basically a tour guide. There were several of us who held this position, because the falls, located about midway between St. Ann's Bay and Ocho Rios, was a popular tourist destination both for those staying in the fancy seaside resorts along the North Coast, coming from as far away as Negril on the western tip of Jamaica and Portland on the eastern shore, and also for the cruise ships, who allowed their passengers to spend a day on land.

I spoke Spanish well enough to be assigned to work with guests from Spanish-speaking countries. I'd help guests purchase water shoes, because the rocks under the falls could be slippery, and show them the beach at the very bottom of the falls where they could dry off and melt into the sand and sun.

When my relationship with Miss Campbell became sexual, I continued to call her Miss Campbell. The lesbian pornography I had watched to help me learn how to be better in bed with Ana could not have prepared me for the experience of dating an older woman. Her fingers, long and slender, gently held the back of my head as she pulled me in for a firm kiss. I'd go willingly, wanting to feel the warmth of her body against mine, the pressure of her lips on my lips. After we made love, our bodies entwined, her fingers traced the outline of my body. I sometimes didn't like my body, wishing I was slender, but when Miss Campbell found the dip of my waist and the rise of my hips, and then the form of my breasts, I forgot about wanting to be slim.

Miss Campbell and I would go to restaurants and sit closely together by the beach so as to feel intimate but without too obviously raising suspicions about us being lesbians. Like I had done with Ana, we talked about moving from Jamaica to a place accepting of our togetherness. Miss Campbell applied for a teaching position in South Carolina. Many Jamaican teachers went to Virginia and the Carolinas for better income and opportunities. I would study computer science at one of the colleges or universities. Our discussions for a life together were interspersed with long poetic rants from Miss Campbell — political, spiritual, and sometimes sexual. She took Amelia's arguments further, adding context and historical background, shaping the point, leaving me in a state of awe at her intelligence.

She introduced me to the concept of generational trauma. How enslaved families were separated. How plantations, wanting to cut the costs of purchasing slaves from abroad, sought out the largest, biggest Black man. He would be the stud and be sent from plantation to plantation — his owner garnering a large profit — to impregnate enslaved women, thus creating an army of children being raised to be slaves.

Though slavery ended in 1834, the impact of slavery did not disappear. Unclaimed children of slave masters, conceived through rape, and newly freed slaves had to learn new ways to find meaning in life and earn incomes. Descendants of enslaved Africans, separated from their homeland and identities, carrying the trauma of enslavement, were thrown into the responsibilities and realities of "freedom."

Beginning in the late nineteenth century Jamaicans started looking for opportunities beyond Jamaica, and thus began the exodus of Jamaicans to places like Panama for the construction of the Panama Canal in the late 1800s, the United Kingdom during the Windrush era, and then the United States in the 1970s.

"These were men and women, raised by parents, grandparents, and great-grandparents dealing with extreme trauma," explained Miss Campbell. "And if they don't heal the trauma, they pass it on."

"Like Daddy's daddy, who left his family to fend for themselves," I mused.

I thought back to my conversations with Daddy about Marcus Garvey and his famous quote, "A people without knowledge of their past history, origin, and culture is like a tree without roots." I remembered the chi chi, the termites, the holes, Daddy had showed me in our colonial buildings when I was little. "We are a people with holes," he had said.

I now understood why Daddy wanted to be a better daddy than his. Why he supported Mommy's education — he was raising daughters he wanted to be able to support themselves, to be strong, to be educated. To have no holes.

Miss Campbell then moved into spoken word, a poem she'd composed about our generational losses:

> My inheritance
> the words you were supposed to tell me ...
> "you are beautiful
> you are loved
> you are smart
> you are creative
> you are an artist of numbers
> you are light
> you are the best part of me"
> ... were never spoken.

"Daddy would tell me that the purpose of having children is to help them evolve beyond us. That with every generation we can fill up our holes ..." I said to Miss Campbell.

"Yes, the holes of pain, our judgments, our biases, our fears and insecurities that keep us enslaved. Playing small, because that is what our ancestors were taught was their place in the world. Our ancestors didn't have the freedom to even have their own stories, let alone keep their own children. But we, hundreds of years later, are still carrying their burdens."

Miss Campbell wrote about finding God in simplicity, in beauty, in love.

> I do not know who I am
> but labels
> put on me
> and that I wear like badges
> but you come
> Always come
> like a warm wind on a still day
> to disturb
> And remind me
> I am something much greater.

But she told me not to despair. And recited another poem:

> Why did you leave us here
> in this cold, dark place
> where it is so hard to find you?
> "Because," you answered, "it is on the blackest of
>   nights that you learn to see."

She talked about how we see God in each other and how we are not whole unless we meet our other half. And to her I was the other half.

* * *

It was a Sunday. Miss Campbell and I were at the church she attended in Ocho Rios.

"You need to tell your parents about us," she said into my ear, while the congregation sang, "Blessed Assurance."

I said nothing.

"You have to," she continued. "It's time."

I knew she was right. I was planning on saving my money from work to move with her come September, which was a few weeks away. I would do anything for her, Miss Campbell. I was totally submissive to her, despite having been more dominant in my relationship with Ana.

I slipped outside. Near a yellow hibiscus bush, I called Mommy and said I had something important to tell her and Daddy. Could they meet me at the church in an hour?

Miss Campbell and I were sitting in a pew near the front of the then empty church when Mommy and Daddy arrived. They smiled when they saw Miss Campbell, and Daddy said he was glad I was getting the support of my tutor.

"But we're perplexed," Mommy began, "why did you call us here? Are you changing to this church?"

"No." I stood up. I took one of each of my parents' hands in my own and told them I was gay.

"But what about therapy?" Daddy asked, taking a step backward. "You said you wanted to stop because you were cured … what about Jerome?"

"As you recall, I never said I was cured. I said therapy was too expensive and I didn't like how the therapist blamed both of you for something that is natural. It is who I am and God accepts that person. He always has."

I recited Psalm 139:113–14 from the Bible: "For you created my inmost being; you knit me together in my mother's womb. I praise you because I am fearfully and wonderfully made; your works are wonderful, I know that full well."

"What is she doing here, then?" Mommy asked, looking at Miss Campbell.

Daddy caught on quick enough, though. He flicked my hand loose and balled his fists. "She did this," he barked, taking a few steps closer to Miss Campbell.

"No," I said, moving in front of him.

"We … we … are in love … I …" I was stammering now, confused. I felt a headache coming on.

Daddy pushed me aside. Miss Campbell rose to her feet. Daddy thrust a finger in her face and started yelling, the church echoing, that Miss Campbell was a seducer.

"I trusted you with my daughter," he said. "God trusted you with the soul of this child … You did this to her. You ruined her."

"No, Daddy, no." I leapt, I charged. For a moment I wanted to go back to when I was a child and we walked the beach and he talked history. I wanted that Daddy who held me on his shoulders. Not this Daddy who saw me as ugly, a sin against God.

I got in the car with my parents. My eyes stained, my head throbbing. I couldn't give up my family. I couldn't live without them. I left Miss Campbell, who'd said barely a word, sitting back down in that pew, a sigh, a moment of time, our hopes gone.

* * *

Home.

Home was a thunderstorm.

Mommy huffed off to her room to pray.

Daddy, saying nothing to me for the longest time, grabbed a white towel at one point and wrapped it around his head.

"Are you really gay, Angeline?" he asked, a murmur.

"Yes," I whispered in return.

Our church might not be one for open lamentations, but if it was, Daddy would surely win top prize. Like a wild animal emerging from inside him, he cried out, a cry that sent shivers through me. He then paced up the stairs to the second floor, down to where I was standing in the living room, down to the ground floor, back up again. Weeping like the image I had constructed of Jacob mourning his son, in Genesis 37:34, or maybe like Rachel wailing, unable to be comforted of the loss of her children, in Jeremiah 31:15.

So loud.

My ears rang.

Latoya began crying, too, and rushed downstairs, either having heard from Mommy directly or overhearing, asking was it true. "Tell me Angeline. Are you gay?"

"Yes," I whispered again.

"You know the Bible seh dis is a sin. Dat you going go hell?"

I closed my eyes then, drifted back into the couch, and just sat, hands sometimes over my ears to block out the noise, the escalating, descending, then rising again noise of Daddy and Latoya, and of Mommy's prayers.

I don't know how long I sat for. I don't know when the endless screaming and crying tapered to a low din, a background noise, but I made my way to my bedroom. Sitting on my bed was Toni.

"I don't care what you are or do," she said, moving toward me, hugging me tight around the belly. "You will always be my big sister. I love you."

* * *

The hurricane came that summer, not without warning.

First rains, light that turned into pellets, that made the zinc roof on the tool shed beat loud, like the drumming of a steel pan. Puddles formed in the backyard just steps away from the back door. The water from the sky morphed into such weight that the banana tree leaves bent under the pressure.

Lightning brightened the night skies.

There were warnings to not go to the beaches, the water was too high, too violent, dropping sea turtles and fish on our shores.

Silence, though, rained down inside our house.

At one point, Mommy asked for me to pray with her. I knelt and asked God for help, for wisdom, for acceptance.

That was all. Nothing more was said between me and God, Mommy and me.

During the nights, in between my broken dreams and wakefulness, I would see my parents standing inside my door frame, praying, mumbling words to God I could not make out. I would moan and turn over, stifling my own sobs in my pillow, knowing they were praying for my soul.

I remembered the Obeah men and women across the island and the rituals they would perform. What if prayer was like Obeah? It only worked if you believed in it? If it only took one person to believe for it to have power? With Mommy and Daddy praying that would be two of them believing. And I feared what they were asking God to do.

CHAPTER TWENTY-ONE

Embracing a love ethic means that we utilize all the dimensions
of love — "care, commitment, trust, responsibility, respect,
and knowledge" — in our everyday lives.

— *bell hooks*, All About Love: New Visions

Daddy had a dream.

> *A crowd of people are swarming our house.*
> *"Send out Angeline," they chant. "Sen' out di dutty
> sodomite."*
> *Some are carrying machetes. Some of the crowd are
> covered in an animal's blood.*
> *Mommy and Daddy run around the house nailing
> the wood that protected our windows during hurricanes,
> but this time on the inside, to keep us safe. The door they
> barred with chairs and a desk.*

But somehow I am outside with the people. The angry people.

I walk toward a deep pit the mob has dug in front of our house. The pit, itself, brought to mind the pit Joseph's brothers dug for him. But unlike the rainwater of Joseph's day, my pit was filled with sharpened stakes waiting to pierce my body.

* * *

Daddy cried after telling me of his dream.

Mommy entered the room then. Her eyes soaked.

Mommy held me in her arms. Like when I was a child, I didn't know where she started and I ended.

"We don't support your lifestyle, Angeline. But you will always be my daughter," Daddy said. "You will always be our daughter."

* * *

Miss Campbell texted.

A text.

She was in North Carolina.

She wrote that all of this with me was too much, too overwhelming.

She wished me good luck with my life.

What about all your talk, I texted back. Of people finding each other in each lifetime, reconnecting because of a promise. Of finding God, and love in beauty, that was us.

What about how you made me come out to my family? How I hurt them?

* * *

I enrolled in Vector Technology Institute in Kingston, to study computer science, having given up on being a minister in the church, a church in America, and getting a degree from an American or Canadian university. Trusting no one. Having few dreams, just surviving.

I started dressing like a goth, wearing dark clothing, a choker with a skeleton, a faux leather wristband, and heavy chains on my jeans.

I met a boy named James at my school who introduced me to 1990s heavy metal music like System of a Down and Slipknot. I saw him one day in the open seating area, tucked away in the back, his black hoodie over his head, a sleeve rolled up exposing his arm. He was doing something, I couldn't see what. I approached, caught the flash of a razor blade against his skin.

I sat beside him and watched him cut. I hadn't cut myself since Ana had gone to Florida. I wanted to feel that release again, to figure out how to hold the blade so it didn't cut my fingers, and where to cut so I didn't bleed out.

I liked James. Or maybe I liked how he helped me find a way to release all the pain, confusion, anguish I was feeling. He knew I was a lesbian. He kept asking me how I could know I was lesbian if I had never been with a guy.

For some reason I trusted him. At least enough to try, *once*. He had a strange masculine yet feminine presence. Maybe it was because of the black nail polish he wore once in a while. His kisses didn't feel gross, not soft and supple like Ana's or Miss Campbell's, but not gross like Trevor's and Jerome's.

When we eventually tried to go further, he was kind. He was gentle about it. When he kissed my neck, I was aroused, but when he tried to penetrate me, it felt like my pum pum closed up and disappeared. All the wetness gone.

I avoided him after that.

* * *

In losing James, I lost someone who could, to some extent, understand me. I needed to speak to someone, anyone, about what my family was going through, my despair, my anger, my losses and betrayals, Ana and Miss Campbell. I found a website for Youth Guardian Services, a worldwide forum for lesbian, gay, transgender, bisexual, and queer youth. A support group of sorts. I wrote about my affair with the older woman, about being in Jamaica where there were no lesbian communities, of my grappling with my love for God, and Christianity, and the churches that denounced me. I met others online who shared similar stories. The vast majority, shunned, becoming ghosts in the eyes of all they love, because to be out came with losing their families and communities. Do you know what it is like to be told that the way you want to love means you will not be granted entrance to God's kingdom?

When the organization advertised for a volunteer position as associate director, I leapt at the opportunity. I wanted to help. I wanted to hear stories. I wanted others to hear my story. I wanted change.

I discovered hundreds if not thousands of young people were crying, dying by suicide, even in America, because their faith said their sexuality was a curse.

I bought a silver ring, in a shopping centre in Ocho Rios, to wear on my thumb when I was in environments I knew would be accepting of my sexuality, to indicate I was out. Complicated, hurting people I didn't want to hurt, lonely, afraid, insecure … but I was out.

This, *this identity* I wanted to wear, to be, to embrace, was no longer just about me and my choices, but about the freedoms of people everywhere.

After several months of listening to the sorrows and the pains of the judgments against these beautiful young people, I decided I should start dating, not give up on finding the one. I wanted to be an example that we can rebound from heartbreak.

Sasha and I chatted a lot via text messages and hung out from time to time. She introduced me to new music like "Ramping Shop" by Vybz Kartel and Spice. The lyrics made no sense for gay people, literally saying being gay was wrong and should be scorned, yet I remembered hearing the song at the last GLABCOM meeting. We seemed to have a knack for taking subtly or explicitly anti-gay songs and defiantly using them for our enjoyment: T.O.K.'s "Chi Chi Man," Elephant Man's "Log On," even Buju Banton's "Boom Bye Bye." I couldn't understand repurposing these types of songs, yet LGBT people had started reclaiming the word *queer* so I guess it made sense.

Sometimes Sasha and I also spoke about the Bible, the anti-gay passages, and the gay-affirming passages.

When I finally decided I wanted to meet someone I had been talking with on a chat line, a girl named Foxxy, Sasha said she would come with me.

"Keep you safe, you know."

"Keep you safe."

EPILOGUE

Change will not come if we wait for some other person or some other time. We are the ones we've been waiting for. We are the change that we seek.

— *President Barack Obama*

After the court case, my way of dealing with the trauma of the assault initially was to take risks, big risks; meeting more and more lesbians online. I couldn't understand myself, the anger inside of me and the tumbling thoughts. I just wanted to escape into the thrill of living on the edge. At times, I hated myself and the promiscuity that temporarily offered some reprieve from my sense of powerlessness from the attack. No relationship lasted more than four months. It was a counsellor, who worked with HIV-positive individuals (youth, women, men, sex workers), who said to me there is no right response to trauma and sexual violence. I needed to be gentle with myself. I needed to be honest with those I was meeting, too; to not put them at risk of feeling emotionally betrayed when I simply was unable to give anything of myself beyond the physical. But most of all, I needed to trust myself, and trust that what I was doing and going through was okay; to pass no judgment.

My faith was the major source of support for me, the Bible, my prayers. Of course, I needed therapy. But having been in ex-gay therapy, I was very afraid of the mental health profession, thinking that my counsellor would want to change me. I didn't know about hypnosis and trauma therapies like Eye Movement Desensitization and Reprocessing (EMDR) until 2019, when I started working professionally with a therapist. I assumed until then that any therapist working within the lesbian and gay communities did so with the objective of "fixing" their patients.

I went to law school, which was a form of activism for me. Through a joint program between the University of London and the University of the Commonwealth Caribbean I was able to pour some of my anger into my aspirations that my studies would lead me to be able to help others like me, and challenge our laws.

I was also volunteering with front-line organizations, which led to my deepening friendship with Jalna Broderick. We had worked together at some of these agencies and we both were concerned with the lack of programming for lesbians. We attended various consultation meetings and workshops for the LGBT community, which we noted largely focused on gay and bisexual men and trans women. We repeatedly asked where was the funding for programs to support lesbian and bisexual women? What support structures existed for lesbian and bisexual women? Simply, there *was* no programming specifically targeted toward bisexual women and lesbians. And that's how Jalna and I started Quality of Citizenship Jamaica (QCJ).

For the first little while, QCJ was unregistered and just committed to creating a community where lesbian and bisexual women from any socio-economic background or of any age would feel welcome. We had also organized a silent protest for sixteen-year-old Dwayne "Gully Queen" Jones, murdered by a group of people in 2013 for showing up to a dance party wearing women's clothing. Our organization also participated in a protest with Jamaicans for Justice and in the "Love Conquers Hate" campaign by the Human Rights Campaign.

QCJ's action was in three areas: advocacy, education, and research. The first workshop we did at QCJ was around self-defence and included presentations on cybersecurity as well as martial arts techniques. Yvonne McCalla Sobers, a community development specialist, did a presentation on understanding our legal rights under the law.

Someone from the audience approached me after one of my talks. I had been sharing my story, which, for me, was another source of healing. In my speeches, I referred to myself as a victim. The person from the audience corrected me, saying I was a survivor. The distinction between identifying as a victim versus as a survivor was profound. As a victim, my guilt and anger were looming over my head, threatening to push me down. As a survivor, my experiences had not broken me. As a survivor, I was rising, not falling. Was I thriving? No. I was living the best I could, but at least in viewing myself as a survivor, I could step outside the experience, look at it more rationally.

Not long after we founded QCJ, I was invited by the St. Paul's Foundation for International Reconciliation to attend the "Spirit of 76" program, a gathering of LGBTQ activists and allies from countries where homosexual sex, including Jamaica, is illegal. The organization requested a lesbian or bisexual from Jamaica, who was also Christian or had a faith connection. Human rights activist and lawyer Maurice Tomlinson recommended me as the best fit for what they were seeking. With the foundation, I participated in multiple panels on sexuality, faith, and LGBT rights in Jamaica. My international activism got its start thanks to the foundation.

At some point, QCJ was approached to give a presentation to police officers, many of whom worked in various CISOCA departments across Jamaica. I was specifically asked if I could help in the police training, as one of the most important ways to help officers understand, instead of just assume, the experiences of survivors of sexual violence is through our stories. I wanted to drill the message in that they needed to do better when working with lesbian and bisexual women.

Being in law school at the time, I knew how to look up legal records. That's when I found the file for Ronique Raymond's appeal. His *successful* appeal. He had been free since March 2012. He was walking around! He knew my identity. No one, not one police officer, not a single person had thought to warn me, to let me know!

By now, I was living in Kingston, going out very little and studying. But for a while after discovering my attacker was free, I could barely leave the house, and I constantly checked behind me when I did. I had friends, lesbian friends, who before the original trial had offered to go and beat the attackers up so badly they'd never touch another woman or girl again. I told them no. I believed in the justice system. Now I was berating myself for the trust I had placed in our institutions. I wondered, *Did I just get myself killed? I did what I was supposed to do, but the system failed me. Where am I supposed to go now?*

Once I got over the terror that I was being stalked, I knew I couldn't sit idle.

While we at QCJ kept our focus on targeting lesbian and bisexual girls and women with programs, occasionally we were asked to undertake projects that encompassed people beyond our community. Maurice, who became my mentor, asked QCJ to undertake a research project on Jamaica's homeless youth population — "gully queens" as we call them in Jamaica. Our report led to more speaking engagements, including at the Inter-American Commission on Human Rights in Washington, D.C. After hearing Jalna and me speak, Human Rights First representative Shawn Gaylord invited us to speak at several of their events at Capitol Hill for International Day Against Homophobia, Biphobia and Transphobia (IDAHOT).

* * *

As I have aged, my faith has deepened. But my connection to the church, not just mine from childhood but any church, has taken time to develop. When I was in ex-gay therapy, I was no longer in Communion with the Brethren church of my childhood. I don't know what my parents shared with the church elders, but there was a point in time when I wrote a letter to the fellowship and was able to rejoin Communion. It didn't last a long time. I knew that my church didn't support LGBT people, and I did not believe God opposed us, so there was a split between what I believed and my church's theology.

There is a passage in the Bible, Acts 2:46: "So continuing daily with one accord in the temple, and breaking bread from house to house, they ate their food with gladness and simplicity of heart." I understood this passage to mean that all the people who share Communion were to also share similar beliefs. I knew that my views on being a lesbian were very different from other believers, and as a result, we were not in one accord. I could not rightfully receive Communion with my childhood church anymore.

Yet, I still had a deep yearning to be part of a church. I took part in online services and Bible studies with various Metropolitan Community Church congregations and the Cathedral of Hope in Texas that helped me understand my faith in the context of church, not just my relationship with God. Through a course I took with Christ Evangelical Bible Institute, I did a deep-dive into understanding the scriptures and homosexuality. Here, I felt my spirit finally being fed.

* * *

How did I forgive my attackers? Foremost, I had to forgive, because I needed to forgive myself. I didn't feel there was any other way to move forward and to continue on with my own life. If I had held onto the anger, it would have eaten me away. I forgave them because I needed to heal. The anger had such control over me. I had to forgive myself for what happened to me. There was a voice inside me that did believe what some said — that the assault was my fault. This is not a forgive them and forget about it type of forgiveness. Hell no. I have not forgotten. I have forgiven because I needed to do it for myself. As for the harm and trauma Sasha experienced — the guilt of that

I have carried every day since the assault, and I am only just chipping away at that.

* * *

My parents, sisters, and I remain very close. In fact, it was my youngest sister, Toni, who was with me at the Walk for Tolerance in 2010. We were all wearing masks, but near the end, some participants took theirs off. I decided to do so, too, for all the media watching. I will say, and I am sure many readers will identify with this, that while I am welcomed by my family, my inclusion is very much based on "love the sinner, hate the sin." I can never be whole with my parents, as a result. I can't share my heartbreaks or celebrate my relationships with them. Things that are real to me and happening in my life are an elephant in the room. I dream of the day when all of me is accepted.

My closest uncle, Anthony, and I stopped communicating when I was sixteen. It was I who stopped talking to him, afraid that he would be like my parents — loving me but hating who I was. I couldn't risk the possibility that he would let me down, so I cut him off, treasuring the memories of who he is and was to me, loving him so much. I just assumed he had rejected me, so I clung to the past and our times together. In 2017, though, he was diagnosed with cancer. Already the disease had progressed to the point where there were no therapies. He died within three weeks of his diagnosis and we never had the opportunity for closure. My greatest regret in life, which perhaps will be with me until the end of my life, is not reaching out to him, but just assuming his position on who I was. I love him. I always will, and I'm sorry I never trusted him with the truth.

I live in Jamaica and am married to an American woman. However, she cannot live here as my wife. In addition to the homophobia we would face, she would have no recognition under the law as my spouse. I will eventually leave Jamaica to live in the U.S. with her, where our marriage is legally recognized and our relationship protected under the law. I do not want to say goodbye to Jamaica, to my homeland. But I have to. I will always fight, always be engaged, until my community is recognized, legally, morally, spiritually, not just in Jamaica but around the world.

* * *

We will all face difficult moments in life. Some moments will be harder than others and some moments may not be as bad as someone else's. Though we walk alongside others in this experience of life, we cannot measure our experiences in comparison to others. Your story is your own, your fight is your own, and your victory is your own. Whatever you have been through and whatever you are now experiencing, you are strong and you will make it. This strength is not a strength of isolation; it is a strength of knowing that support is available to you whether through family (of birth or of choice), friends, faith community, or therapy. You've made it this far and I know, believe me, I know how hard it's been to get here, but there's so much more ahead of you.

Continue to show up in this world as your full self, if it's safe to do so, or identify a safe space where you can have that authenticity. By your very existence, you are changing lives. The power of one person is not about individuality. Rather it is about how we individually make an impact in the lives of others, and how they make an impact in others' lives, and so on. The power of one person is how we use a component of who we are, or our experience, to benefit someone else. The power of one person is how each of us as individuals can come together to collectively make a difference.

You are a powerful co-creator, you are fierce, and you are beautiful. Go shine your light.

ACKNOWLEDGEMENTS

This book has been an idea since I mistakenly wrote a ten thousand–word essay for an undergrad assignment. And in 2016, after Maurice Tomlinson introduced Susan and me, this idea became a draft proposal.

While I had hoped this book would have been a reality from then, the years in between have given me time to collect more stories, remember events, and look at the past through different eyes.

Thank you, Ms. Davis (one of my high school teachers), who saw me and saw something in me. By directing me to the St. Ann Parish AIDS Association, she expanded my world.

I remember with gratitude Youth Guardian Services, those who started and led the organization, the board of directors, and the friends I made from that email listserv. Angela and Rob, thank you for being queer siblings across the distance.

The Q Christian Fellowship (formerly Gay Christian Network), thank you for being a place for solace, spiritual support, and comfort during one of the worst times of my life.

Rev. Canon Albert Ogle and everyone involved in making The Spirit of 76 a reality, thank you for the experience and opportunity.

Maurice, thank you for seeing my potential, encouraging me to speak out, and giving me the opportunities to do so.

To the lesbian and bisexual women of J-FLAG and Women4Women who paved the way, my deepest gratitude and thanks.

My love and thanks to the adults I claimed as surrogate parents and relatives, Donalda and Douglas, Diane and Rhonda, Lindy and Rick, Hilaire, Auntie Yvonne. Jalna, you have had many roles in my life since we've known each other. Thank you for being a consistent source of support, helping me recall the stories I've shared, listening to every crazy thought that had potential (and those that didn't), even at 2:00 in the morning, and all the ways too numerous to list that you have been a part of my life.

Thank you Kenita Placide and Kasha Nabagesera, powerful activists, who I watched and learned from.

The members and ministers at Founders Metropolitan Community Church in Los Angeles, thank you for helping me reconnect to my spirituality. Special note of love and thanks to the Rev. Camille Rodriguez Araullo.

Thank you, Reece Ford, for helping me remember that there were other LGBTQ youth who still had an interest in faith and matters of the spirit.

I am particularly grateful to every organization and individual that gave me a platform to share my story and the realities of LGBTQ life in Jamaica, provided direct or indirect support, helped with collecting my thoughts, and edited my writing

(Human Rights First, Los Angeles LGBT Center, Advocates for Youth, OutRight Action International, formerly IGLHRC, and more). Thank you also to every individual donor and funding organization for your support of QCJ.

Rev. Adam Dyer, thank you for being a friend and constant small voice asking me about my lingering interest in being a minister.

Damien Williams, my brother-friend, minister, fellow social justice advocate, and author, thank you for loving on me.

Despite our disagreements, I'm grateful for my family of birth (my parents and sisters), who loved me as best they could and who instilled in me strength, pride, and fierce determination to stick to my values and beliefs.

The issue, or maybe it's my fear, with writing names in an acknowledgement for the impact on your life years prior is that sometimes you don't remember everyone's name. If you are not named, your impact has not been felt any less nor are you any less important than those who have been named. You each hold a special place in my heart, and I am forever grateful for your presence in my life and the way you have impacted me. Because of each of you, I found the courage to speak out. Because of you, others can find themselves on these pages. Because of you, others will know that they, too, can speak.

Thank you.

ABOUT ME

I am a 2014 graduate of the international Emerging Leaders program at the Los Angeles LGBT Center, which organizes and empowers individuals to defeat anti-LGBT prejudice locally and through hands-on mentorship with activists from around the world. I received a 2014 Hero Award from the St. Paul's Foundation for International Reconciliation for my work on LGBT rights in Jamaica, the 2016 Troy Perry Medal of Pride, and the Florida Youth Pride Coalition, International Youth Icon Award in 2017.

Over the years, I have presented at various events and panels including the Inter-American Commission on Human Rights, the National Gay and Lesbian Task Force "Creating Change," Founders Metropolitan Community Church's "Realizing the Right to Relate," Washington University's World Affairs

Council, the Salzburg Global Seminar in Austria, Human Rights First's IDAHOT events on Capitol Hill, D.C. (2014–2016), Intimate Conviction in Jamaica, and the Ethics of Reciprocity: Theology intensive retreat in South Africa. I have published several writings on the LGBT situation in Jamaica and have been quoted and interviewed for numerous media outlets and books.

I am a fellow of the Salzburg Global LGBT Forums "Strengthening Communities — LGBT Human Rights & Social Cohesion" and "The Many Faces of LGBT Inclusion."

I am the 2020 Christianson Family Scholar at Meadville Lombard Theological School where I am studying for my Master of Divinity degree. I also serve the Neighborhood Unitarian Universalist Church in Pasadena, California, as the intern minister. My LGBTQ activism continues in the work I do preparing reports and serving as an expert witness on asylum cases for LGBTQ Jamaicans.